RASTA
LIVITY

A Basic Information Text

by

Kwende Anbessa-Ebanks

KWEMARA PUBLICATIONS

First published, 1983
SECOND EDITION, 2004
by Kwemara Publications
PO Box 4902
London SE5 7EL
E-mail: kwende.kwemara@btopenworld.com

ISBN 1 872121 04 7

Layout by Rastafari Devon Stewart
Typeset and Printed in Britain by
RUZ Comprint

Table of Inclusions

By virtue of His Imperial Blood, as well as by the anointing which He has received, **THE PERSON OF THE EMPEROR IS SACRED**, *His Bignity (dignity) is inviolable and His Power is indisputable...*(Art. 4: 1955 Revised Ethiopian Constitution)[1]

I Acknowledge inspiration for this publication from:

* Almighty I Jah Rastafari, Haile Selassie I, The Head Creator, without Whom I can do nothing worthwhile. I give thANKHs.

* I Parents, Family and Ancestors - Aunt Fanso, Jah Bless.

* I & I Rastafari of The Ethiopian World Federation, Inc., especially Ras Tinish and Ras Lion for their acknowledgement and assistance. Thanks Sis Sonia for your typing, Ras Devon at RUZ typeprinting, and Bingi Zema for the drumming drawing.

* Queen Lady Theresa "Isis". ThANKHs for sharing, for being there, and for your proofreading. Stay Blessed.
* Bro Ian, Sis G, and all supporters of the first book.

THIS BOOK began as a five-page information sheet, written in 1982 to meet the appeal from young and old, of all races, for information on Rastafari Livity. This publication marks a trinity of celebrations this year: 1. the Golden Jubilee (50th) Anniversary of Jah Emperor's Visit to Britain (14 October, 1954), 2. my own Golden Jubilee year, and 3. the 21st anniversary edition and first re-issue of this book since it was first published as a 30-page booklet in 1983. I have gratefully added suggestions from readers of the first book.

"While life goes on, the teachings must stay strong, for every day a new born tells us we can't surrender." D B, stay blessed.

Ah Baraka; Amesegene (ThANKHs and Praises). Rastafari Guidance.
A labour of Jah Love: Ras Kwende, 2004

SPEECH: A GLOSSARY OF TERMS USED

The 'overstanding' of word, sound and power is important to all relationships and achievements. Different word-sounds have their own vibrational power and effects. It is psychologically better for one's language to be compatible with one's ideology and world-view. Therefore, I and I (our) Afrikan Language, called *Kwankwa* in Ethiopian Amharic, and *Iyaric* in Rastafari speech, is very important for us.

In the English language, the word "I" best expresses the fundamental unity of Iration (Creation). The pure and essential aspect of mankind, and the common principle upon which Creation depends for its maintenance is the I. This Spiritual Being is the Ultimate Living Companion and Sustainer from Ras Tafari, the Head Irator. She is pure and essential nourishment; the Sustainer in natural raw foods and, of course, the essential Godly life force.

Members of Rastafari are keen that the I, inspired through RasTafarI, Haile Selassie I, will influence the way we think and act. The I stands for the collective oneness, while the u/you bends to self and selfishness. So, the I replaces the word "you", while 'you-sounding' words, which generally begin with the letter 'u' or 'hu', are replaced with an I sound. Certain other words are modified to express truth, life, extended familyhood, essential Godhead, and to remind us of the focus we need to maintain for a positive existence. Examples are:

Rasta Usage	English
Jahnoy, Jah, Jahovah	Our Emperor, Father, God
HIM	His Imperial Majesty, Emperor Haile Selassie I
I	The pure, essential aspect of Iration, which is in mankind
A one	One (personal) or 'you'.

Babylon	Places and people of wickedness and "downpression"
Bignity	Commands to a proud and respectful existence. (Dignity, otherwise)
Bongo	Afrikan Black
Churchical	In a church or ceremonial setting
Crelove	Create
Dawta of Zion/Dawta	Rastawoman/Daughter, or Woman
Downpress	Oppress; to unjustly dominate a one's will and humanity
Dread	Great, heavy, hard, righteous wrath, dreadlocks, fearsome
Dreadlocks	Afrikan wool grown naturally and freely, without combing, thereby producing "Nattydread-locks"
Forward	Back, backward
Green, Gold and Red:	Order of the colours in the Ethiopian flag, which is how it is referred to in HIM's 1955 Revised Constitution[1] and the EWF constitution. These Afrikan national colours represent, uppermost, **Green** the strength and life of the Afrikan (+ Hope) **Gold** - with the Lion in it - is the sun and our mineral wealth (+ Charity) and **Red** - the blood of our innocent and our ancestors, which was shed in defence of I and I liberty and prosperity (+ Faith). Also selected is **Black**, our colour, the blessing of the sun, strength, purity and correction. Jah made light out of the darkness (Psalms 18:11). Carbon, the black element, is the foundation of all living and ex-living things.
Heartical	Sincere, earnest

Hola	More complete and pure than "holy"
I and I (I n I, I&I)	We, us, our. Of Rastafari family
I-call	Remember, recall
Icept	Concept
Idren	Brother, Brethren in Rastafari
Ilect	Elect
Iliver	Deliver
Imanity	Humanity
Initation	Meditation
Inity	Unity
Ipatrilove/ Repatrilove - see *Repatrinate*	
Iration	Creation, celebration.
Irie	Of joyous Irits; "upful", a greeting
Irit	Spirit
I-story	History (his-story excludes I and I glory)
I-tal	Natural, righteous, pure
Iver	Ever
Ivine	Of God; divine
Iwah	Time, era, hour, dispensation
Jah	God, The Head Maker unidentified, but Jah RasTafari identifies HIM.
Kinghead	Husband
Livity	Way of life
Lion	The Crowned Lion is one of I & I most famous symbols. He has the cross over one shoulder with an Ethiopian flag (see Green, Gold & Red) billowing over him. He stands in the central, gold area on the original, main flag. His Majesty uses the Lion (*Anbessa*) to represent Afrika and His Own Majesty, Strength and Nobility. His Official Titles include "The Lion of the Tribe of Judah". Lion and Lioness also refer to I and I the Sons and Daughters of Rastafari.
Man and Man	More than one Rastaman

Natty	Knotted, matted, coiled up Afrikan wool (hair), dreadlocks
Negus	The King
Ones and ones	People; more than one person
Overstand, overs	Understand
Queen	Wife, Rastawoman
Ras	Head, Prince or Duke. Also title of a Rastaman.
Rastabet/Rastafaribet	Rasta House of meeting; tabernacle
Repatrination	To return and rebuild one's nation; repatriation (sounds of "hate")
Selah	Amen; an acknowledgement or closing endorsement, used in prayer or writing
Sistren	Sister(s) in Rastafari
Strong	One week, i.e. of 7 days
Tabernacle (taba)	Temple, church, house of worship
The I	You
Wisemind	Wisdom
Wool	Afrikan type of hair
Yesus Christus (Ethiopic)	Jesus Christ
Zion	Heaven

ቀ፡ኀይለ፡ሥላሴ፡ንጉሠ፡ነገሥት፡ ራስ፡ ታፋሪ.

"Haile Selassie I; King of kings, RasTafari"

Some Rastafari Greetings

RASTAFARI:	The most forthright acknowledgement / greeting by Rastafari , expressed on meeting and on departing.
BLESSED / BLESSINGS: (*Baraka*):	(Same meaning)
GREETINGS:	(Same meaning)
GUIDANCE:	Departing with wishes for RasTafari Blessed Guidance.

HAIL / HAILE:	Acknowledging someone in The Name of RasTafari.
HAILE I:	A forthright Rastafari acknowledgement or greeting.
I-I:	Acknowledging one's essence.
IRIE (IRIE I):	Uplifting one's spirit on meeting and departing. Also means "Nice".

Rastafari would rather greet with the word "Hi!" instead of "Hello". 'Hi' is uplifting one's spirit, whereas "Hello" is conjuring the lowness of hell.

Spelling note:
AFRIKA /AFRIKAN

The 'k' spelling of Afrika /Afrikan is used in respect to how the vernacular or traditional languages on the motherland pronounce the word, with a strong vocal 'k' sound rather than a 'c' sound. Secondly, modern pan-Afrikanists (global Afrikanists) have adopted the 'k' spelling as part of the Afrikan affirmative world-view.

Pan-Afrikan, or global Afrikan, thought focusses on the fundamental oneness of the Afrikan experience, whether we live in continental, homeland Afrika or in the experience of the "Carry-beyond" our Afrikan border, otherwise called the Caribbean.

"Spiritual and Cultural Education leads them again into Inity on the national as well as on the personal level."
(Haile Selassie I Speech)

"I am because we are and because we are therefore I am"
(Ancient Afrikan Wisemind)

A BRIEF I-STORY OF RASTAFARI IN ENGLAND

Since the late 1950s, Rastafari have been grouping together in England, and London in particular. Most groups were communes for the teaching and practising of Rastafari Livity. The main areas from which Rastas first came to public notice were Ladbroke Grove in the west and Brixton in the south of London.

The Universal Black People's Improvement Association (UBIO) was established in 1969 to help Black People maintain their bearings in a hostile and racist white society which was downpressing and persecuting them at all levels. UBIO was modelled on Marcus Garvey's UNIA organisation and comprised mainly of members from Shepherds Bush and Ladbroke Grove in west London; and from the south, Mayall Road on the then "Brixton Frontline", and Battersea, as well as from north London.

Out of UBIO came Emperor Yohannes Local 33 branch of the Ethiopian World Federation, Incorporated (EWF), an Afrikan organ that was formed in the USA in 1937. Local 33 was established in Portobello Road, west London, on August 25, 1972 as a sub-local of EWF Charter 37 in Jamaica. On 24 May 1974, with approval from Ethiopia, Local 33 established the first branch of the Ethiopian Orthodox Church (EOC) in England, in Ladbroke Grove. Members were mainly Rastafari who were

St Agnes Place HQ, London

already members of the Rasta tabernacles. However, in 1975 and 1976, many left the Church because of ideological differences with the priest over the wearing of dreadlocks and the Ivinity of I and I Creator, Emperor Haile Selassie I.

Local Rastas from Mayall Road and from Battersea established the early tabernacle at numbers 26 to 34 St. Agnes Place, Kennington, south London, in 1968. This House came to be regarded by many as the focal point for Rastafari activities in England. But its story is one of a trying and difficult transition. The five houses were long empty and unused by Lambeth Council, the local government, and the Brethren occupied them for their religious and community uses. The other houses there were already squatted in by white, middle class rebels.

At that time, however, the nation was very open in their racist persecution of Black People, and Rastas in particular. Several brutal attempts were made to evict the group from the houses, while the white squatters were left undisturbed. Their gas and electricity supplies were cut off; the fire brigade smashed down the doors and "mash down" the houses, making numbers 26, 30 and 32 derelict. Armed police with ferocious dogs terrorised and beat up the youth and woman folk. Brethren were dragged off to prison for further beatings and to be forced drugged. Sistren suffered miscarriages and other illnesses due to police brutality. One event was graphically captured in a film called "Rasta Ina Babylon" by Black film producer, Howard Johnson.

Around 1974, Rasta elders, led by Ras Pepe Judah (Menelik), Ras Binghi and Ras Malachi, founded the British headquarters of the Jamaican organisation, the Twelve Tribes of Israel at St. Agnes Place. By 1979 though, with ideological disagreement, a large group of Brethren and Sistren had left St. Agnes Place and had taken the name "Twelve Tribes" with them. However, the founding members and others remained and set up an administration named Rasta International HQ (RIHQ).

But it soon became apparent that, although Rastafari was rapidly growing in number throughout the earth, centralisation was still lacking. Inspired by two of Haile Selassie I Utterances, **"Goal Unity"** and **"Action Now,"** the members held a seven-day seminar, ending 23 July 1980, on Unity and Repatriation. However, this was not so successful so we planned an international conference for the following year.

But the problems continued. The London Electricity Board again cut off our electricity supply and our street lighting on a false claim of unpaid bills. Various tactics were used to delay return of our supply so we had to plan the conference in dim candle light in what became known as "The Black House". Throughout the previous cold weather, adults, youth and babies gathered around the paraffin[2] cooker/heater in the kitchen at No. 28, to avoid the cold drafts from the damaged houses.

Despite the obstacles, by the Grace of Rastafari, our International Conference of Rastafari and other Afrikan-conscious people was held at the Lambeth Town Hall, Brixton, London, on Thursday, 23 July (HIM's Earthday) 1981. All the national Rastafari Houses attended, except for the Twelve Tribes of Israel. Organisations attending were, Rasta International (the hosts); Rastafari Universal Zion (RUZ); Tree of Life; Rasta Unity; Mind, Body and Soul, members of Homeward Bound, and members from Emperor Yohannes Local 33.

The Conference was reported to be "an unprecedented and a successful event". Many people saw Rasta Drumming and tasted Ital cooking there for the first time, free of charge. This was the second major conference of Rastafari in England, the first one was that organised by Emperor Yohannes Local 33 at Loyola Hall in Tottenham, north London on 11 January 1975. However, this 1981 Conference brought to the fore the issue of Rastafari addressing functional Inity and working through their local groups under the umbrella of one organisation to manifest this Inity. In this way it would be best able to address mass repatriation and all other issues necessary to I and I livity.

Conference resolved to set up an umbrella organisation to maintain and develop Inity and to help to achieve Repatriation. At the suggestion of Ras Ammanuel 'Pinto' Foxe, the sleeping Ethiopian World Federation, Incorporated (EWF) was re-activated in England for this purpose. A national Executive was

A view of the audience and Conference drummers, Brixton Town Hall, London, 23 July 1981.

sworn in on Thursday, 27 August 1981 at Rastafari headquarters, St Agnes Place. Jah Bones of RUZ was voted in as the President of the national umbrella. However, it was clear that effective centralisation within EWF needed a better overstanding of functioning a large international body in alien and hostile societies, as well as knowledge of the EWF's history and reasons for its past slumber. Members at St Agnes Place opted to research into both the EWF and repatriation so we set up the Repatriation Research Committee (RRC) for this purpose. The membership also mandated Rasta International to function as a sub-committee of the EWF, to carry out works requiring liaison with the local council authorities and report back to the EWF.

At St Agnes Place, we also set up the New Flower Dawn (NFD) project to continue our community welfare work. This was despite refusal from the government Charity Commission to register us as a charity, with all the benefits available to charities at the time. The HQ's activities included prison and hospital visiting, Rastafari drumming and chanting, counselling, and community feasts and functions on Rastafari Holadays, all given free of charge and on a self-help basis.

However, in 1981, New Flower Dawn applied to the government for funds to renovate the Houses, which they had "mash down," and also necessary funds to continue our community works, some of which was also their national responsibility. Only £75,000 was allocated instead of the three hundred thousand pounds (£300,000) we claimed on official, professional advice. NFD agreed to set up a hostel for homeless Black youth who were considered to be "at risk" of becoming criminal or mental. This project depended on renovation of the Houses and had to be met from the £75,000 allocated. However, the HQ has long since returned to being maintained on a self-help basis.

Back in May 1982, the RRC received a call from the EWF Pioneer Settlers Corps (PSC) in Shashemane, Ethiopia. They felt that an official visit from members in England would offer them strong moral support and would also enable I and I to research and publish the Land Grant, and the Repatriation programme. Plane fares were quickly raised by all EWF Locals in England and a two-man delegation left the HQ on Tuesday 28 September, 1982, returning with a report on Sunday, 5 December 1982. Since then, more members have successfully repatriated, and several building and developmental projects have been established or projected on the Land.

One of these projects arose out of another call, which the RRC received in February 1985. This was a crisis call on behalf of Colleen Reid, the 16-year-old daughter of one of the Settlers. Colleen suffered from a congenital heart disease, which, by then, needed urgent life-saving attention. Heart surgery was requested and the organisation started immediately to fund-raise. Our efforts raised fourteen thousand pounds (£14,000), out of which we flew Colleen over to England in November 1985 for a successful operation and subsequent recuperation.

Reasoning at Rastafari Universal Zion (RUZ) in Tottenham, London, 1980s. Ras Menelik (Pepe Judah) is in the foreground of the picture.

Special valuable assistance in this venture came from the Jamaican Nurses Association, the West Indian Ex-Service Men's Association, also the Black Press, with an admiringly positive report by Bro. Tony Jules. There was great support also from the Jamaican High Commission, and all contributors and helpers who made the effort so successful in so quick a time.

The EWF continued the effort and worked towards improving hospital facilities on the Land. For example, one year later, in

October 1986, members and volunteers completed a sponsored walk of the 876 miles from John O' Groats in the northern tip of Scotland, to Land's End in the southern tip of England.

In November 1985, when Colleen Reid arrived in England, a court case had just ended which involved some EWF members, but primarily, Seymour McLean. Bro McLean was in prison serving a nine-month sentence on a charge of stealing over one thousand books, worth over eight thousand pounds (£8,000), from various British National Libraries. In fact, these books represent the priceless thousands of ancient Ethiopian books, manuscripts, and religious treasures looted and stolen from churches in Magdala, Ethiopia, by the British army in 1868.

Further, it was Bro Seymour who brought his possession of these books to the attention of the police, so that the issue of looted Afrikan heritage would come to public attention. According to him, he had "liberated" Ethiopian history with the books from the British Museum and other national libraries, because, "the youth must know the truth about their past." This event helped to renew and strengthen the international call for the reparation of Afrikan artefacts and heritage stolen by European pirates. It was also the subject of a tv documentary drama at the time, called "The Book Liberator".

1. RASTAFARI, THE PREAMBLE:
A REDEMPTION LIVITY

RasTafari is more than a religion. It is I and I Livity of Ivine Inspiration and Incient Righteous Tradition; it is I and I Total Way of life, based on Peace, Love, Purity, Truth and Justice, which are all represented in the Personage and Embodiment of His Imperial Majesty, Emperor Haile Selassie I, RasTafari, Jah Almighty of Creation. It is not a cult, sect or an -ism. Rastafari is the revealed livity from our great ancient Afrikan Tradition, giving relevant guidance for today and for the future. It is that which I and I live and express through our culture as loyal Afrikans.

Rastafari gives I and I pride and the strength to persevere and overcome the trials and tribulations of life without resorting to wickedness and injustice. I and I proclaim Haile Selassie I as God, without any apology. Through HIM we gain our path to justice, redemption, salvation and prosperity.

Emperor Haile Selassie I, aged 5

2. STATE OF THE NATION

Rastafari Livity first emerged outside of Afrika in the Caribbean Island of Jamaica where it was rejuvinated and reconfirmed by The Coronation of Ras Tafari, Negus Tafari Makonnen as His Imperial Majesty (HIM) Emperor Haile Selassie I of Ethiopia-Afrika in 1930. Certainly there was need for a people, the Afrikan People, after the European attack with slavery and attempted genocide, to dig deep into its own soul in order to rise above the gravest of threats to its legacy as the Guardians of Creation, but more so, to its own survival. Where would they find this inspiration if not from their own Ancient Order of Livity, previously unknown to the rest of the world? Rastafari Livity is the modern manifestation of that same Ancient Order.

Let us remember that the chattel slavery and attempted degradation of Afrikan Black People over the centuries began with the Arabs. However, they were ousted and replaced extensively by the Europeans who practised these evils with a greater vengeance. There is still an attempt to subjugate Afrikans into a neo-slavery, and with this new-slavery idea comes con-cepts such as "politically correct" rather than "morally correct". Much has already been said about the atrocities committed against Black People during the crusade of the abuse of their trust and hospitality. This was done primarily to impose chattel slavery, colonialism and "apartheid" on Afrika. But the Afrikan Spirit cannot be crushed, so psychological means were intensified to make the injustices seem more "politically correct".

Many large corporations of the former "slave owners" continue using deceit and economic intimidation to pirate and exploit the natural resources and minerals of Afrika to enrich themselves materially. They continue to exploit Afrikan ingenuity, exper-tise and labour to build up a technology which becomes a tool to further exploit and downpress Afrikan peoples. They continue to persecute and imprison Afrikans disproportionately in prisons and mental institutions where they beat, force-drug, and murder them. The endeavour to brainwash and demean global Afrikans with a biased education, propaganda and religion is still strong. So also is the desire to continue the subtle and blatant hijacking of Afrikan cultural and religious expressions, while trying to deny their great contribution to the enrichment of the world.

As a result, many Black people are still ashamed of their ethnic origin and skin colour. They desire or pretend to be white, regardless of being brown in shade, or part white, or of the darkest hue of Black. Some bleach their melanin-rich dark skins with cancer-causing chemical creams. Some want their hair to be more European and less woolly Afrikan, so they burn it with hot iron-combs or chemical creams as if it's something to destroy. When they also reject their Afrikan speech and names they finally reject themselves and their human bignity (dignity).

Yet, at the start of the 21st century, some high profile European white women are injecting *collagen* material into their lips to get that "luscious, full-look beauty", as well as other forms of cosmetic surgery to look more ethnically Afrikan. They also now, often begrudgingly, acknowledge the Afrikan woman's full and firm bottom as a desired beauty. Obviously, then, the wise and loyal person will find glory within the heritage granted them by Nature at the command of The Head Creator. So the Rastafari grow their Afrikan "natty dreadlocks" with pride, defiance and as a symbol of the love of self first.

For when a people slavishly accept encouragement to grow to hate themselves, they become their own worst enemies - the enemy within. The downpressor can then rely on them to be an obstruction to their own national progress, as well as to become killers of their own people. The negative power of self hate!

The confused Afrikans react in the same way, be they in Afrika, the Caribbean, America, Europe or Asia. The British society has, in recent times, finally admitted to practising disorientation tactics against Black People, calling it "institutional racism". Many call it white racial injustice. The nature of it depends on where in the world Black people live, on what proportion of the population they occupy, and on how deeply countries with black puppet governments obey their masters' voices by remote.

There are those whites (and other peoples) who still fear offending God and know that racial and all injustices and downpression are wrong. However, whilst their efforts at ending such behaviour are praiseworthy, we ourselves must be determined at gaining and maintaining our liberty and prosperity. This requires for us to be alert and Inited, for His Majesty Says:

"It is not the strength or the power or the determination of those who oppose us that will delay success in this battle, but only the weakness of our unity." (Utterance: "Find Solutions").

Should we fail to gain meaningful unity, annihilation awaits us. But meaningful, functional unity first has to overcome all the selfishness, the self-hate, and the slavery and neo-slavery programming causing havoc in the world today.

It is out of this crisis, of over four hundred years, that Emperor Haile Selassie I has come to deliver the Afrikan People. This deliverance crucially helps us to rediscover I and I essential self, not only on a political, but also on a cultural and a spiritual level. We must now stand firm in His Ivine Name, in His Majesty, and in His Example to pass His test of time and circumstance. In this wise, we will all abide in peace, prosperity and **collective security** under His Iternal Redemption. In this Redemption we shall enslave no-one, and none can harm nor enslave us anymore.

ETHIOPIA FROM CREATION

The River in Eden/Ethiopialand

The Garden of Eden is reported in the Bible (Genesis) to be where mankind first began. From there, Jah settled each nation of people into its own portion of land. To the Afrikan People He gave the special guardianship of original Eden.

So where is Eden? A River watered Eden, and from there it became four branches. The first branch was Pishon, which watered Havilah (North East Afrika and Arabia region). In Genesis 10:7 Havilah is the son of Ethiopia/Kush. It is also the ancient Kushite district of Northern Ethiopia, the region now called Eritrea. The second branch is Gihon (Abbay, Gihyon or Blue Nile) and it waters Ethiopia (Kush). The third and fourth rivers, Hiddekel (Tigris) and Euphrates are also in the Ethiopian and Arabian region of the earth.

Therefore, Eden is in the continent of Ethiopia/Afrika, and specifically in the country of Ethiopia.

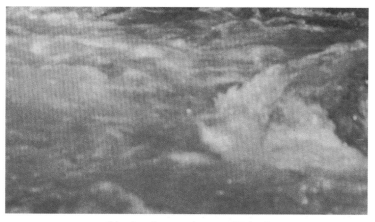

"And a river went out of Eden"

Ethiopia is therefore the world's first nation, as indicated in Genesis 2: 7 to 15, and proven also by several prominent archaeologists. Over the decades, they have been making repeated finds of the oldest human bones in the area.

The Egyptian part of the River Gihon is now called the Nile and "The Mother of the Jordan". The modern Ethiopian part is still called Gihyon in some areas, but is generally called the Abbay or Blue Nile.

Egypt has been called "Ethiopia's Oldest Daughter" and was Ethiopia's cultural centre before she fell, in association with foreign nations and customs. Ethiopia, Kush, Egyptos, Abashinia, Abesha, Abashanti, Kamit and Afrika are all words for Black. Afrikan Black is, historically, the only way that the early Europeans represented Baby Jesus and His Mother, Mary – the "Black Madonna and Child".

Ancient Greek historian, Herodotus, and others, wrote that Ethiopia ruled at least part of Greece and India. The River Ganges in India is named after an Ethiopian King who ruled parts of Asia up to that river.

Israel's special favour with Almighty RasTafari is because they were of Ethiopian descent. They were Ethiopian-Afrikan Black People. Read Amos chapter 9:7: "Are ye not as Children of the Ethiopians unto me, O Children of Israel? Saith The Lord." Regarding Ethiopia's special relationship with The Lord, read Psalms 68v31; Psalms 87; Jeremiah 13v23, Genesis 2v7-15 and Amos 9:7. The Falashas are of the original Jews who returned to Ethiopia from Jerusalem with the son of King Solomon and Queen of Sheba, Menelik I, and the Ark of the Covenant.

Many people of West Afrika have always traced their ancestry via Egypt to Ethiopia, the world's first civilisation!

3.   EARLY RASTA I-STORY AND GROWTH

From the earliest days of the modern chattel slavery, over 400 years ago, there has been those of I and I who have always remained true to our Ancient Order of Afrikan Livity.

Although the Maroons of the hills of Jamaica are famous as staunch resisters of slavery, who brought the British slavers to their knees in 1738, it was the more Monastic Hillsman, with whom they were often associated, who maintained the strongest link with our Ancient Way, the way of Ancient Ethiopia.

Through this mystical link, and also through inspired study of the Bible, the Hillsman Brethren knew of the Divinity of the Ethiopian-Afrikan King who was to come for Black Redemption and Regulation of mankind; He who is now revealed as RasTafari, Negus Tafari, Haile Selassie I. This they preached before the birth of Marcus Garvey, that shining Black Star who arrived later. The Hillsman were therefore the first rejuvinated and re-emerged Rastafari, through whose inspiration Marcus Garvey became empowered to preach their doctrines, which he had by then become one with.

Marcus Mosiah Garvey was re-incarnated (born) on 17th August 1887 in the parish of St. Ann, Jamaica. He was a direct descendant of the Maroons. From an early age, Papa Garvey was in the forefront of the defence in the war of freedom and justice for the Afrikan Race.

In 1914, Prophet Garvey founded the Universal Negro Improvement Association (UNIA) in Jamaica. Its motto was: One God! One Aim! One Destiny! Its aims were Black Pride and Bignity, Inity, positive development, and Repatrination Back-to-Afrika; "Afrika for the Afrikans, those at home and abroad."

In 1916, Mosiah Garvey went to America and established the first of many branches of the UNIA. Soon the international membership rose to five million. In 1918, Garvey founded a weekly paper, 'The Negro World', with international circulation in French, Spanish and English. In 1918, also, Garvey founded the Black-conscious, Afrikan Orthodox Church. In 1919 he set up the Black Star Line Shipping Company, partly in response to discrimination against Black passengers on white-run ships, partly to link up the world's Black People and as a future vehicle for repatriation to Afrika. Garvey also established the Negro Factories Corporation and the Black Cross Nurses.

However, the forces of Babylon reacted. In 1927, after years of harassment, the American Authorities framed, imprisoned, and deported Prophet Garvey back to Jamaica. Yet, although he was by now very weakened, this great man persevered to work for the liberty of our People, inspiring Elders Nkrumah, Kenyatta, Malcolm X, Mandella, Azikewe, Lumumba and Nyerere.

Earlier, in "Philosophy and Opinions" (volume 1, chapter 3) Prophet Garvey said of the Afrikan Race:

"...We have handed down a civilisation through the ages which has been claimed, exploited and abused by a morally weaker people who, like ourselves in the past, are forgetting their God and making a mockery of Him. The time is near ... when our princes shall rise to bless and glorify the true and living God. Surely the Negro shall put the world to wonder in the REVELATION OF GOD THROUGH THE RACE".
And again:
"If the white man has his idea of a white God...We as Negroes have found a new ideal...We believe in the GOD OF ETHIOPIA..."

Prophet Garvey echoed the Rastafari Hillsman earlier teachings when he told a Kingston congregation after his return from America in 1927:

"Look to Afrika where a Black King shall be crowned for the day of our Deliverance is near."

This prophecy was fulfilled on 2 November 1930 with the crowning of Haile Selassie I of Ethiopia. His full title, His Imperial Majesty, Emperor Haile Selassie I; King of kings, Lord of lords, Conquering Lion of the tribe of Judah was, to many people, further fulfilment of biblical prophesies in **Isaiah chapter 9 verse 6, Daniel 7 v 9, PSALMS 87 v 4, 1 Timothy 6 v13-15, Revelations 17 v 14; 19 vs. 11-16 and Revelation 5 vs 3 + 5:**

"No one in heaven or on earth or under the earth, was able to open the book or to look into it... Then one of the elders said to me, 'Weep not: behold, the Lion of the tribe of Judah, The Root of David, hath prevailed to open the book, and to loose the seven seals, thereof...'".

It was followers of Garvey in Jamaica who became best known for preaching that Haile Selassie I is that Black God and King of Ethiopia whom Garvey often spoke about. All three of the earliest preachers were harassed by the police and sent to jail.

The first and most prominent of these early preachers who taught that Ras Tafari, Haile Selassie I is the Godhead was Papa Gong-g'un Guru Maragh, otherwise known as Leonard Percival Howell. Born in 1891, Papa Gong was a world traveller who spoke several languages. In the early 1930s, in St. Thomas, Jamaica, Bro Gong (Howell) started preaching the Divinity of Emperor Haile Selassie I. Because of this he was jailed in 1934 for two years on charges of sedition and blasphemy. In 1940 Bro. Gong changed location and purchased an old estate near Sligoville, in the hills of eastern St. Catherine, where he established a community of the King of kings of Ethiopian Salvation Union called "Pinnacle".

It was at Pinnacle that Rasta Livity and the first Rasta Government developed, amidst constant police harassment and brutalisation by order of the British slave makers in Parliament at Westminster, London. The Idrens were finally forced out of Pinnacle and into the Kingston ghetto area called Back-O-Wall or Shanty Town in 1954, before its demolition in July 1966. (The area later became known as Tivoli Gardens).

Bro Gong (Howell) published, in 1936, a book of spiritual instructions called *The Promised Key*, under his spiritual name, G G Maragh (Gong-g'un Guru Maragh). As a world traveller, and knowledgeable about Afrikan languages, Papa Gong was likely aware of the following meanings: *G'un-g'un* - matted wool-hair (dreadlocks) and plaits (Ethiopian word); *Guru* - a man with more than one wife (Shona-Azanian word). Bro Gong

Gong-g'un Guru Maragh (Leonard P Howell)

had more than one wife. *Mara(gh)* means 'now', or 'in this time', or 'so it is' (in Swahili - East Afrikan). *The Promised Key* seems to have been inspired by *The Royal Parchment Scroll of Black Supremacy*, published by Rev. Fitz Balintine Pettersburgh in 1926, but the Gong's book was written specifically to glorify The Emperor Haile Selassie I Ivinity and His Empress Menen.

Joseph Nathaniel Hibbert was born in Jamaica in 1894 but around the age of 17 he went to live with his father in Costa Rica, where he spent some twenty years. During this time he owned and ran a banana plantation there. He also became a Master Freemason as well as the President of the then Local 81 branch of the UNIA. After his return to Jamaica in 1931, Bro Hibbert started to preach in the parish of St Andrew that Emperor Haile Selassie I is the Returned Messiah. He then moved to adjoining Kingston and was encouraged to find that Bro. Howell, also, was already preaching His Majesty's Ivinity.

Young Tafari (aged 11) and His Father, HRH Ras Makonnen

Bro. Hibbert's organisation was called the Ethiopian Coptic Church. He was later, in 1948, a founding member of the EWF in Jamaica, Local 17.

The third of the earliest Haile Selassie I Ivinity preachers was a Jamaican seaman, H. Archibald Dunkley. He set up an organisation called the King of Kings Missionary Movement, through which he continued to preach his doctrine. However, at the time, Dunkley did not see HIM as God Himself, but as the Son of the Living God. Significantly, though, Rastafari writer, Ras Everton McPherson later wrote: "The author can attest to the fact that before Bro Dunkley's death in 1986, he had adorned himself with the sacred locks and hailed His Majesty as The Almighty Creator."

In 1948, Bro Dunkley was also one of the founding members of the first local of the EWF in Jamaica, Local 17.

4.   WHO, WHAT AND HOW RASTAFARI IS

RasTafari is Haile Selassie I. Rastafari is I and I spiritual and cultural, religious way of life, or "Livity". Rastafari Livity is founded on **L**ove, **I**ntegrity, **V**irtue, **I**nity and **T**ruth, **Y**ielding to His Ivine Will for Rights and Responsibility, and Peace and Prosperity. Rastafari is I and I who are, as is said in Isaiah 43:7, *"... every one that is called by His Name"* - **Ras Tafari** Makonnen, Haile Selassie I, Emperor of Ethiopia, Abba Jahnoy, Jah, I and I God and King. Jah is the Highest, most Perfect Man. Check Genesis 1v26 and 27, and the biblical History of Yesus Christus (Jesus Christ). The majority of people (i.e. the men as opposed to Man) have strayed from the Holy, Man-is-Jah Truth and now need to recognise the Fatherhood of Jah and the spiritual Brotherhood of Mankind in order to find their true self and become again one with the Ivine-I.

The Emperor Haile Selassie I, aged 16

From ancient times, before the birth of Yesus Christus (Jesus Christ), the nations of the world had fallen to paganism, barbarianism, and worshipping stones or other inanimate objects. But Ethiopia-Afrika has always maintained a Faith established on the ideals which some men today call Christian. Centuries later, when the Faith of Ethiopia started to spread due to the writing of the Bible and then the works of Yesus Christus, it became evident that certain nations were trying to corrupt the Righteous Afrikan Teachings of the Bible and of Yesus Christus. After the Ethiopian Eunuch met the Apostle Philip and tested his knowledge (Acts chapter 8v27) he learned how widely and diversely the Original Afrikan Faith had been translated, especially later with the influence of Rome and its empire. The Ethiopian Holy Fathers then decided to establish a more organised and regulated religious body or Order so as to righteously influence the corrupted bodies and at least, to keep them from completely leaving the true path.

This Order is recorded in history as being confirmed in the 4th century AD and is today called the Ethiopian Orthodox Church (making Ethiopia the oldest Christian kingdom in the oldest civilisation). Yesus the Christus (Jesus the Christ) said that no man could get to The Father but through Him (John 14v6+9). EthiopiAfrikans have, since olden times, sought the Christ Spirit. Now, God The Father has been Revealed to I and I **Rastafari** through the Personage of HIM, Emperor Haile Selassie I. All Afrikans are spiritually able to receive and to manifest this Revelation, too, but some have to first break free of their psychological chains of white slavery and downpression. For, even though European versions of Christianity and the authority of the Bible remains strongly influential on Afrikan people in general, basic biblical proofs of HIM's Divinity (see chapter 3) are, nevertheless, still rejected by them without consideration. They struggle, therefore, in obeying the Ancient Call to Afrikan Consciousness and Inity which this Revelation entails.

31

Rastafari is loyal to the Inity of the Afrikan for our own benefit and for global prosperity. Despite a seasonal and opportunistic public pretence by many people to love Rastas, such as Bob Marley who has gained international acclaim, they still fight against Rasta. Rastafari cause people to feel uncomfortable with hiding from themselves in churches and other institutions of religion. Rastafari speak out truths and rights, impartially, against wrongs and lies. This may cause offence but is not a sin. Rasta stand for being true to thine own self, hard as it can be, for the truth shall set us free but living a lie is a big burden. RasTafari Haile Selassie I Says that education and the family is the key to progress and prosperity. A Great Family Man, The I Majesty took the Office of Ministry of Education under His Personal Charge within His Government. One's first foundation for education begins in one's family.

True education is greater than merely academic (partial) learning. Learning the skills of Life and relationships with people is the greater knowledge. This means that we must accept that all good skills are important and complementary in society. Therefore, no one is superior or inferior. The higher good of human endeavour is to be Ivinely inspired by each other – to acknowledge that the skills or actions of this or that person were well done, delightful and encouraged us to greater hope and endeavours.

True education is that which leads us to accept our own good, including outward traits such as, for us Blacks, our strong woolly hair, our melanin rich dark skin, and our lovely full lips, as well as our soulfully rich and soothing singing voices, our irrepressible creative genius, and our deep and uplifting spirituality. These are what the Creator deems necessary for making us special in our complementary roles in the world.

I and I Rastafari are the keeper and Ifender of our Ivine Heritage of truths, rights, and essential worth. RasTafari Is.

Rastafari is I and I Mission:

After leaving Jamaica with my sister and brother in April 1966, and being, myself, absent for a very long time, I finally was about to return for the first time, with the help of RasTafari. I had not made any great plans beforehand because, after all, I was going "home". However, I was apprehensive about the type of reception I figured I might receive as a Rasta. In this I was responding solely to the reaction of people in general to Rasta, worldwide, as well as from my own personal experience in England at the time.

I arrived in the yard of my Grand Aunt ("Aunt Fanso" Imogene Lyons). She was our guardian during the two years before our parents were able to send for us to join them in England. I was now a grown man and pleased to be present before my Grand Aunt in my new appearance, but nervous because of it. Would she recognise and welcome me with a joyous embrace or would she tell me that I can't stay there, or what? She looked me from head to toe, and back again. Then she spoke. "So this ah yuh mission!" "Yes, Aunt," said I, with great relief. Bless you and may your Ancestor-spirit continue to guide with Jah Grace.

i.   The Jahhead (Godhead)

Lightening and thunder heralded the Reincarnation (Birth) of The Godhead in this *Iwah*. Ras Tafari Makonnen, Negus Tafari Makonnen, Great Grandson of King Sahla Selassie, was rein-carnated as Lidj Leul Tafari on Saturday, 23 July 1892 at Ejarsa Goro in Harar Province, Ethiopia, East Afrika. His Father was the Royal Ras Makonnen, hero of the Battle of Adwa and cousin and valued counsellor to Emperor Menelik II. His Mother was Weyzaro Yeshimabet ("Lady of a Thousand") who died in child-birth, aged thirty, some eighteen months after HIM's Birth.

The Baby Tafari's Birth ended four years of terrible drought and famine which had brought death and darkness to the people of Ethiopia. At the moment of His Birth, the lightening and thunder which accompanied HIM was sweet music to the people; for **rain** came again, bringing them hope, once more. A new era had just begun.

The young Tafari was Sanctified (blessed/baptised) and named in a church ceremony on His fortieth day. Here He first received His baptismal name of Haile Selassie I. However, He was called Tafari, His Birth Name, until His Coronation thirty-eight years later when He again used His baptismal name, Haile Selassie I.

In November of the same year of HIM's birth, 1892, a great light, since then called Holmes Comet, appeared in the heavens[3] and was interpreted as an omen, fulfilling the biblical prophecy of Isaiah 9 vs 2 to 6:

*"The people that walked in darkness have seen a great light; they that dwell in the land of the shadow of death, upon them hath the light shined...they joy before Thee according to the joy in harvest...**For unto us a Child is born, unto us a Son is given, and the Government shall be upon His shoulder; and His Name shall be called Wonderful, Counsellor,** The **Mighty God**, The Everliving Father, The Prince of Peace. Of the increase of His Government and peace, there is no end..."*

His Majesty began this process of Government at the young age of thirteen. In 1905, then as Lidj Tafari, His Highness Ras Makonnen promoted Him to become Dejazmatch ("Keeper of the door") a district Governor or Chief of Gara Mulata province near Harar. Months later, Ras Makonnen fell sick and died in March 1906. In May 1906, Emperor Menelik II called Dejazmatch Tafari to the capital in Addis Abeba and appointed Him Governor of Sellale. At fifteen years of age He was appointed Governor of Baso and at seventeen, He became

Governor of Sidamo Province in southern Ethiopia. However in order to further His education He obtained permission from the Emperor to only take a part-Governorship in the province. In 1910, aged eighteen, He was appointed to the prized Governorship of His native province of Harar.

In July 1911, in His twentieth year, came another turning point in Young Tafari's Life. Dejazmatch Tafari married Weyzaro Menen (Walatta Giyorgis) and together they produced six children. This was a marriage made in Heaven; it showed the example of complementary wedded partnership and family life. How lovely are the words of His Majesty regarding their relationship:

"During our companionship, We never had differences that needed the intervention of others... Our wishes were mutual..."

1st Crowning

In 1913, after the passing of Menelik II, his grandson, Lidj Iyasu succeeded to the throne. However, his arrogant and irresponsible behaviour was unacceptable to the majority of people, and when he tried to change Ethiopia from a centuries-old Afrikan Christian state to a Muslim one, they deposed him on 27 September, 1916. Princess Zawditu, Menelik's daughter, was crowned Empress, and Dejazmatch Tafari became Ras Tafari, having being **Crowned** Regent[4] and Heir to the Ethiopian Throne. At age 24, it was considered that Ras Tafari could wait a while longer to become emperor. His new title was now His Highness Ras Tafari Makonnen, Crown Prince of Ethiopia, with responsibility for the work of the government.

In His provisional reign as Regent, Ras Tafari developed plans for Ethiopia's advancement, balancing her traditions with, and adopting the best and most progressive ways of modern life. Indeed, His maxim is: **"Progress must be Moral."** His far-sightedness, courage and shining social and political reforms have made Him eminent in world history. Much of the advances He made were achieved with His own money, in addition to that of government. Money was merely a tool for HIM to use in His Charge of Ethiopia's collective benefit, as shown by His Sojourn at Bath, England, in 1937: **"Our Life at Bath was very hard. We encountered great financial problems. The media had reported that We had taken a great deal of money with Us when We left Our country and they were attempting to make people believe this; but it is a complete lie. We took what We thought was sufficient for a certain time, but even that was soon finished as We used it to help the exiles."** (HIM Autobiography page xiv of vol.1 & page 36 of vol.2)

Other early national improvements made by His Majesty during His Regency included revising the legal and penal system; establishing and improving printing presses to provide low priced books and papers of educational value to the people; reorganising the national finances and establishing the Bank of Ethiopia with His own money in 1928 and, introducing educational exchanges of young people with other nations, as well as establishing diplomatic relations with foreign countries.

His Majesty also effected many improvements to existing services in the country, which included the health service, the army and police force, as well as establishing a national anthem. He brought welcome improvements in the work of the clergy, as well as established the sovereignty of the Ethiopian Church. He also improved communication, in particular roads, telephone, telegraphic and postal communications. Most of all, His Majesty improved the working conditions of the people, abolishing feudal rule by the landed gentry in favour of appointed rulers of merit. At the same time, He successfully set about a gradual abolition of domestic slavery, which Ethiopia had in common with several Afrikan and Middle Eastern countries. However, in domestic slavery, as different from chattel slavery, slaves could own land and even businesses. They could even marry into their keepers' family. But with progress, even this form of servitude should cease.

On 28 September 1923, in pursuit of international **"collective security"**, His Majesty accomplished getting Ethiopia into membership of the League of Nations despite opposition from racist, imperialist members, except France. This made Ethiopia a founding member and the only independent Black and Afrikan member country, the others being the majority white members.

2nd Crowning

On 7 October 1928, then aged 36, Ras Tafari was **Crowned** a second time, this time as Negus (King), "without ceasing to be Heir Apparent and Regent Plenipotentiary". Queen Zawditu remained Empress, until her passing on 2 April 1930.

3rd Crowning

Then, on Sunday, 2 November 1930, Negus Tafari Ascended the Imperial Throne of Ethiopia at His **Coronation** as *Negusa Negast*, meaning King of kings, or Emperor. Kings, rulers and envoys of 72 different nations from all over the world went to His Coronation to pay HIM homage. Another *Iwah* had begun.

His full official Ethiopic[5] title is: *Moa Anbessa Zemnegeda Yihuda, Girmawi, Kedemawi Haile Selassie, Seyume Egziabher, Negusa Negast Zeityopya.* He is also *Janhoy (Jahnoy), Abatachin Hoy, Yegetewotch Geta, Berhan Alem.* All these titles mean, His Imperial Majesty, Emperor Haile Selassie I (First Power of the Most Hola Trinity); King of kings, Lord of lords, Conquering Lion of the tribe of Judah, Ilect of God-Himself, Light of this world, earth's Rightful Ruler. I and I know HIM as God Almighty Head Creator, without apology, Jah...Ras Tafari.

This Coronation made His Majesty the only person to be

Crowned three times (a hola trinity of crowning), and made HIM the 225th monarch in an unbroken Line of Kings from the Union of the Black King Solomon with Queen Makeda, the Ethiopian Black Queen of Sheba. This union is related in the Bible, 1 Kings 10 verses 4, 5 & 13 and in the ancient Ificial Istory of Ethiopia, *Kebra Negast* (Glory of Kings). See also Article 2 of the 1955 Revised[6] Constitution of Ethiopia, as well as the Introduction to HIM Autobiography.

Their Imperial Majesties at Coronation Ceremony, 2 November 1930.**"During our companionship We never had differences that needed the intervention of others. Our wishes were mutual."** (HIM)

His Names are evolved from the Ancient Ethiopic Tongue which was forerunner to ancient Coptic-Egyptian, Hebrew, Arabic[7], Ge'ez and its modern derivative, Amharic, with its own script or writing symbols. The English translation of His Ivine and Royal Names and Titles are:

Haile Selassie I	Power of the Holy Trinity, The First and Only, The I AM (of Exodus 3 v14).
Ras Tafari	Head Creator; Maker of everything (Ras is Head, Prince or Royal Duke)
Abatachin Hoy	Our Father (The Heavenly One)
Dejazmatch	Commander of the Door (a provincial governor or chief)
Inderase	Regent
Janhoy	Your Ivine Majesty (affectionate term for The Emperor Haile Selassie I)
Lidj Tafari	Child or Prince of Creation
Leul Tafari	Prince of Creation
Makonnen	High Ranking Nobleman
Negus Tafari	King of Creation (Negus = King)
Negusa Negast	Kings of kings (or Emperor)

Some Female Titles:
Itege is 'Your Beloved Majesty' (affectionate title for the Empress). *Li'ilt* is Princess, and *Weyzaro* is Lady, or Mrs (a married woman). *Weyzerit* is a young or unmarried woman.
Nigeste Negestat is Queen of queens; Empress.

King Alpha & Queen Omega
In the coronations of former times, the emperor's wife was crowned empress on a separate day, after the emperor's crowning. Now His Majesty was mindful of educating the People into the fullness of Familyhood, which begins with true Partnership and Inity of Husband and Wife. He, therefore, had His Queen, Weyzaro Menen, crowned *Nigeste Negestat* (Queen of queens, Empress) in the same ceremony following His Own Coronation. They are King Alpha and Queen Omega in Iverliving Inity.

39

Ras Tafari is His Ivine Office and Haile Selassie I His Holy Name. Although there are men called Tafari and Haile, and others surnamed Selassie, there is Only One bearing the full Name of Jah (God) Ras Tafari Haile Selassie **I**, The First and Only. Haile Selassie 1st and His Last in One Iternal Inity.

To assist Him in the task of "the Government upon His shoulders", His Majesty promptly Granted Ethiopia's first written Constitution on 16 July 1931 (Constitution Day). This outlined and explained the rights and responsibilities of every citizen in the Realm for the first time. It was later revised and expanded in 1955. In 1931, also, His Majesty had scholars complete and present to Him an Amharic translation of the Bible from Hebrew, Greek and old Ethiopic-Ge'ez.

This Haile Selassie I Bible has 81 books (15 more than the edited and overwritten King James European translation of 66 books) and is a more true representation of the Mind of God. However, Italian war delayed publication, except in photocopy form in 1936. Following this, on His Earthday in 1961, 23 July, His Majesty Granted and published the Revised Amharic Bible for the people, reminding them, **"We in Ethiopia have one of the oldest versions of the Bible..."** (See chapter 15 on HIM Utterances).

Earlier, in 1951, after years of negotiation, His Majesty achieved the independence of the Ethiopian Church from Egyptian rule. For the first time since nearly a thousand years of church history, Ethiopia had achieved her own Patriarch, called the "Abuna". Then in 1962, His diplomacy achieved the re-federation of Eritrea with Ethiopia. On 25 May 1963, with Ghana's Kwame Nkrumah and Afrika's other leaders, Emperor Haile Selassie I established Ethiopia as the centre of the newly formed Organisation of Afrikan Unity (OAU) of which He was the main architect. May 25 thus became known as Afrika Liberation Day.[8]

In April 1966, the Emperor made a historic Visit to His People in the Caribbean (Trinidad on the 18th, Tobago on the 20th and, Barbados and Jamaica on Thursday 21 April). In His Speech, He reminded the Jamaican Parliament that Jamaicans and Ethiopians are **"Blood Brothers"**.

Yet, despite all these benefits which His Majesty brought to Ethiopia, the people were not satisfied. In 1974, they rebelled against His Government and tried to kill HIM. However, this was an event that He had expected and planned for. Yes, the time had come to confirm the schemes of mankind and to give new lessons and Revelations to the ignorant. Like the sun behind the horizon or behind the veil of the clouds, His Imperial Majesty mystically disappeared and veiled Himself within Ethiopia. No more "Lamb to the slaughter", as is said about His previous Revelation as Christ the Son. Now He's the Son and The Father with His *Hola* Force, His total cosmic unity of the Trinity; The Conquering Lion who shall break every chain and "give I and I a victory, again and again" as the song says. Jah Ras Tafari Haile Selassie I is Supreme. He cannot die for, He is Everliving.

Likewise, Rastafari are no martyrs to be devoured in the arena of wickedness by evil men. Instead, I and I come as Noble Lions and Lionesses to defeat spiritual wickedness and to earn the right to live forIver. I and I bring a final revelation and correction. No more false doctrine of being martyred or crucified and buried. Instead, people must crucify and bury their own negative characters. So Rastafari focus on the benefits which The Emperor has brought to ÆEthiopia and the world.

I and I seek to maintain complete Inity with the True and Living Godhead, Haile Selassie I, Ras Tafari. Indeed, He is our Inity. One Jah, One Righteous Aim and One Destiny. Remember that Ras Tafari is one of the Personal Names of HIM Emperor Haile Selassie I Jah Almighty. He is I and I Inity.

Emperor Haile Selassie I is Inspiration for Afrikan Independence and Sovereignty, a Symbol of Afrikan Inity, and the Father of world peace and **"Collective Security for Surety"**. Let HIM be praised.

ii. Man and Woman and the Family

The Ras Tafari, Emperor Haile Selassie I and His Queen, Empress Menen, Whose marriage together brought forth six children, are the Supreme Example of a Family. And so, as RasTafari is the Head of Christ and Men, likewise Man is the head of Woman (1 Corinthians 11v3; Genesis. 1v20-23 and 3v16). However, there is not superior and inferior; instead, there is **complementary relationship**. RasTafari makes Man and Woman to complement each other sexually, physically, emotionally, spiritually and in the roles they must perform - they are building units of Creation.

Man represents the active principle of the universe, specialising the physical work like ploughing the fields in which he sows the active seeds. Woman represents the passive principle that nurtures the seed and the young plant to produce the fruit of the field. She bears the future generation within her. In spiritual Inity with each other, man and woman both add greatly to the protective force of I and I Family. Man's duty is to guard his family, to provide for them and to guide them with compassion, through just and righteous examples and teachings. Woman is responsible for the domestic care and provision for her family and her household - the Afrikan Woman is the "Queen and Mother" of *I*ration. She is a partner in the education and welfare of her family. In her maturity, she becomes "Queen Mother".

Man should maintain a high level of self-discipline in order to be the ultimate vanguard of God's Iration. He is not to pursue behaviour associated with a woman, nor is a woman to behave as a man. They should not wear the clothes that pertain to the other gender (Deuteronomy 22v5). Adornment, such as earrings and a mass of vanity jewellery are not fitting for a Rastaman.

The Rastawoman covers her head in public and before a man who is not her husband or close family. She dresses modestly, covering herself in bignity with a garment that extends well

Rastafari Queens in Regal Dress

below her knees. This shows how she wishes to be regarded. Some women in cold climates claim that wearing trousers keeps them warm. The answer to that given by a visiting elder is that what a woman wears *under* her **dress** is her business and noone has to see it. Therefore, what is worn and shown is what your gender can be said to own, so to speak. The best model for Rastafari dress is a traditional Afrikan cultural one, with no corruption but with specific male and female regal choices.

Pleasing to Jah RasTafari is the man and woman who encourage and glorify their spouse in the bignified grace of their gender. Cursed is he who abuses the bignity of his woman's sexuality where he should be Ifending her.

Woman was made to be virtuous and modest. The Rastawoman is not a vulgar or a brawling speaker; she keeps her business respectable. She has only one kinghead (husband). All this is part of keeping her modesty as well as the protection of her royal bignity, personality, and her feminine sexuality, like unto Empress Menen. For more on the virtuous woman, read the counsel given to King Lemuel by his mother in Proverbs chapter 31 vs 10-31.

During her monthly period of blood flow, i.e. during normal menstruation, a woman must exclude and confine herself indoors, as much as possible, from personal and social interaction for 7 days, even if bleeding ceases before this time, which is normal. For example, if actual blood show starts on say, a Monday, confinement goes on to Sunday, so that on the Monday following she should return to normal duties. This confinement helps her to properly complete her cycle of bodily and spiritual regeneration and preparation. It is an Afrikan and biblical tradition, necessary for preventing a clash and interference with the spiritual balance of others during her menstruation, recouperation and regeneration. During this period, the woman is exempt from sexual intercourse, from cooking for her husband (see also Leviticus 15v19) and from attending the tabernacle and churchical functions, but should still perform her Ivotion to RasTafari.

Apart from the needs of very young infants for their mothers, it is good that where possible or convenient, the father of the family should have some time to cater to the nutrition of the family. During the mother's confinement is a good time. After all, many men say they are soldiers and during soldiering times they have to cater for themselves. This, of course does not take away the proper roles of children of the family who are old enough to administer their household duties.

And now, remember that it is better to choose one's partner with one's spiritual I, together with the physical eye, rather than with the carnal eye alone. Total communication, that is, in words and spirit, is necessary for all good and successful relationships.

So,if you find yourself having to criticise, remember to give praise when it is due (including to yourself, too). Everybody, regardless of status, gender, race, or religion, has ways about them that are praiseworthy. Be aware, look out for them and acknowledge them. Selah.

Children

> *"Lo, Children are an heritage from the Lord;*
> *and the fruit of the womb is His reward."*(Psalms 127v3).

Children are our **Posterity for Prosperity**. They are the future of our race and the purpose for our endeavours. Parents, do not provoke your children to wrath, and children, obey your parents in God; honour your father and your mother (Ephesians 6v1-4, + Exodus 20 v 12). It is by being obedient to parents and respectful to elders that children gain true protection in later life.

Parents, remember that each of you have **responsibility** for your children, therefore you both have **rights** to them.

Teach your children focus and responsibility by giving them household duties to complete and to achieve therefrom. *Train up a child in the way he should go and, when he is old, he will not depart from it* (Proverbs 22v6). Know the whereabouts of your children at all times, to the best of your ability. It is not a responsible parent who chooses not to give a good amount of their time (quality time) to their children, but to give them toys instead. Toys are a good aid in children's development, but quality time from the parents (especially the mother in the early years) is essential.

When we love our children we will bring them up with guidance and discipline tempered with reasoning, compassion and justice. If we fail to bring up our children with proper discipline, we would expose them to the colonial social workers, the police and the penal system to deal with them. Therefore, take responsibility for our children and thereby, please our foreparents and RasTafari Almighty.

NAMING CEREMONY (SANCTIFICATION) OF THE RASTAFARI CHILD

Sanctification of I and I Daughter of the Most High

In the RasTafari Tradition of the King of kings, and in the Bible (Leviticus 12:1-5) after giving birth, a mother remains confined indoors to recover with her baby, away from all labouring work. This confinement would last for forty days (six weeks) for a boy and eighty days for a girl. After this time, the baby is ready to be name blessed (sanctified /baptised) in the assembly. A suitable name having been chosen for the child, the name blessing ceremony formally welcomes him/her into the community.

Although the priest facilitates this Rastafari blessing, it combines the strength of the family and friends, young and old, in the assembly, thereby, giving everyone a role in the event. This ceremony also strengthens the spiritual and cultural traditions of the nation-community. Therefore, the foreparents (ancestors) are reverenced at this time also.

On the day of the ceremony, usually before sundown, a table is set out and dressed with water, coconut, fruits, nuts, honey, salt, oil, incense and flowers. These are tokens of a rich and bountiful reward of the newborn, and hope for a sweet future. They are blessed by the priest during the ivotional prayers. Readings include Psalms 128 and the Ivine Utterances of Almighty Emperor Haile Selassie I.

The ceremonial blessing of the child and naming takes place during his/her immersion (baptism) in the blessed water containing herbs. It continues with his/her tasting of bitter nut or fruit, and honey/sweet. These remind us of the patience and perseverance necessary to overcome difficult times, and the sweetness of prosperity, the reward for good living. The child is then anointed with oil (such as olive) to encourage a smooth and healthy passage within life, as exampled by HIM's own Naming and Coronation ceremonies.

The assistant parents make their pledges to assist the parents in the upful raising of their child, according to the Ivine Principles of Rastafari. The parents also ask for the Ivine guidance in their parental role. All children in the assembly are collectively blessed in sharing the day with the new baby. A baby-welcoming chant is raised before the ceremony is sealed with prayer.

RASTAFARI INITIATION-AFFIRMATION INTO YOUNG ADULTHOOD

In Afrikan Tradition, the initiation of children into young adulthood is a crucial part of national education and confidence building. It begins usually around age 12 or 13 but can sometimes be earlier or later, or when a girl sees her first menstruation. Thereupon, she undergoes a ritual washing after 7 days.

The rite of passage prepares a young person to apprecilove the rights and responsibilities of adult life – the need for self help and occupational work, self awareness and social rights and responsibilities, all within the reverence of Almighty Rastafari. It reassures the young person that the community acknowledges and values their transition into adulthood. It gives them a sense of purpose and belonging, of total mental, spiritual and material wellbeing. In order to be worthy of these rights and responsibilities, the initiation seeks to instil in these young people qualities such as bravery, obedience, patience, perseverance, justice, morality and the resultant pride in achieving.

Year of preparatory activities
During this time, the candidate undergoes training in spiritual awareness, self-discipline and self-assurance. They may also engage in family history re-creation, and maybe some community service.

He or she keeps a special portfolio (journal / logbook) with pride. In it they enter what is agreed by responsible adults, as well as their own pictures and writings of what life has taught them during the year of passage.

Separation
The passage takes the child through a mental-psychological and spiritual rebirth. This involves them being separated for a while from their usual environment (a type of confinement) under the tutoring of an elder of the same gender, their 'gender tutor'. They then return home as new and maturer individuals. Because of the need for academic education, it is good that this separation takes place on a vacation from school.

Under his or her 'gender tutor', the candidate also completes a one day fruit-and-water-only fast, and engages in "adult reasoning" about life and about man-and-woman relations. He or she then finalises their "graduation speech".

Several youth of the same gender may be initiated at the same ceremony. Readings are taken from the Ivine Utterances of Emperor Haile Selassie I, and from the Bible – Psalms 119. The candidate is then blessed with water and anointed with oil. An appeal is made to Almighty Rastafari, I and I Foreparents (ancestors), Parents and Elders, asking them to bless and Ivelop the candidate's Irit of Wisemind, Knowledge and Overstanding, Justice, Patience, Perseverance and Prosperity.

The candidate then proceeds with their gender tutor along the aisle under a green-gold-and red canopy of adulthood to the chant "Enter into His Gate". He or she is then crowned and presented with a Scroll or Gift of Attainment. After receiving words of guidance from adults in the assembly, and gifts, the newly affirmed young adult makes his or her graduation speech of attainment.

Sex and Birth

All types of sodomy (homosexuality) are prohibited as being anti-humanity and anti-Traditional Afrikan Livity. Male complementary to female sexual intercourse is God's Law. See also Leviticus 18 and 22. The New Testament also upholds this principle: *"Effeminate, nor abusers of themselves with mankind shall not inherit the kingdom of God."* (1 Corinthians 6: 9+10).

Abortion and other forms of murder are also prohibited for the same reasons; God commands us to populate the earth (Genesis 1v28) and this is by a man to woman sexual union.

However, there must be discipline and self-control within sexual relations between man and woman. For example, Commandment 7: "Thou shalt not commit adultery," meaning, do not go with the mate or spouse of another but your own. Also, no sex with under-age persons, no incest – no sex with close relatives, or other unholy forms of sex. The Bible, Leviticus 18 v 6 to 30 gives more.

According to the *Fetha Negast*[9] of Ethiopia, marriage is primarily a mutual agreement between a man and a woman to bond together and assist each other in the work of life, to raise children therein and, to enjoy the blessings of sex. It is best for this commitment to be ceremonially confirmed in a wedding at an assembly of members of the community.

Man should not sexually know a woman during her period of menstruation, while she is bodily and spiritually renewing her being. So-called bad luck and weakening of the body will result from breaching this barrier, as well as VD and other diseases of the penis and vagina.

Marriage and sex within the race promotes the strengthening and rebuilding of the Afrikan Family. But even so, it is the better to choose a mate with the spiritual, thoughtful eye and the physical eye, rather than with the physical or carnal eye alone.

iii.   Livity: Life, Reincarnation and Existence

Life is the pinnacle of Creation. Destruction of life came into the world through men's folly, vanity, recklessness and wickedness. RasTafari "creloved" us all to be ever living; He takes no pleasure in men's destruction. Therefore, Rastafari seek to live forIver. This is our birthright, provided that we live according to Jah's Ivine Laws, with right livity, right practices, right nutrition and right relationships. The spiritual and cultural way of life, of right, as followed by Rastafari people is called *Livity*, and in particular, *I-tal Livity*.

Death and its associations are avoided by Rastafari whenever possible and practicable. Life and life-sustaining associations are pursued in deed, thought and language. Thus, life-words are preferred to those that sound of death. So, for example, "dedi-

50

cated" is changed to "livicated", from the root word "Livity". The Rastafari will, therefore, generally seek to avoid the mourning of corpses and the glorifying of funerals or other celebrations of non-life. We prefer to support and comfort the living and to honour the noteworthy living memory of those who have passed away in the flesh. Non-life is a hypnotic doctrine preached by killer Babylon. See also Numbers chapter 6v6, Psalms 115v17-18 and Matthew 17v1-13.

Rastafari know that hell is on earth and, likewise, the Kingdom of Heaven is also on earth but can only be experienced by those who are godly and, therefore, also living. "God is not the God of the dead, but of the living." (Matthew 22v32). Too much fear of facing the next stage of life will delay your progress and lead to a lack of hope, and to despair. One then seeks to escape through fantasy and denial and/or over-sleeping, even unto death. But there is no true death, so people who die are reborn, by a method called **reincarnation**, and given another opportunity to make good and to get it right. This is expressed in Afrikan names such as Babatunde, meaning "Father has returned".

Regeneration (reference Matthew chapter 19 verse 28) is a progression on reincarnation for it is an everliving Inity and cooperation between body and spirit, to renew life again and again. However, one has to live to the highest standards of a disciplined livity to achieve this.

"His flesh shall be forever fresher than a child's; he shall return to the days of his youth." (Job 33v25).
*"Enoch was translated (*taken up alive) *that he should not see death..."* (Hebrew 11v5).
"Who satisfieth thy mouth with good things; so that thy youth is renewed like the eagle's. (Psalms 103v5).
" And all the days of Methuselah were 969 years." (Genesis 5v27).

The motivation for living a certain disciplined way of life comes from the rewards which one obtains and expects from following such a course. His Majesty Says: **"The preservation of health is a duty..."** (Important Utterances, page 260).The strongest of us will, at times, waver from the straight and narrow path. Sickness and other personal crises are times when one's urge to re-enter the straight path of behaviour is often at its peak. They are times when people often strongly seek to "get their lives back into order", to re-claim their Livity. Their food is a crucial element within this quest.

iv.   Food, Nutrition and General Health

The basic principles of Rastafari Traditional nutrition are written down in the Bible (Leviticus 11; Deuteronomy 14, and Numbers 6). Although some Niahbinghi Rastafari eat fish, and even less of them eat meat according to the Nazerite and other biblical codes of diet, the ideal is *I-tal* vegetarian.

I-tal refers to a natural, just, clean and righteous living as well as to the food which we eat to aid us in this way of life. I-tal also refers to the mode of preparation of food, which maintains it from being tainted by non-Ital substances and vibrations. The healthiest state to be in is one of balance with Nature, i.e. to be **Natural**. The natural products of Mother Earth and Nature, i.e. fruits, grains, vegetables, water, the sun and air, provide well-being for mankind and are termed as **Vital**. Unifying the concepts of I, and Natural, and Vital, we arrive at **I-tal.** A person who practices the I-tal culture is called an **"I-talist"**.

The nearer to the natural state that foods are prepared and eaten, the more I-tal they are said to be, and this means no animal meat products, strictly no pork, and no shellfish or meat, no creeping things, no insects and no liquor. Most members of the Niahbinghi Order eat only I-tal food, cooked with traditional

Afrikan spices if required. As salt is already present in natural foods, I-talists do not normally add extra raw salt to their food. Most foods, in general, naturally contain enough salt for good health. Additional salt retains water and cannot be absorbed into the body. It therefore irritates the tissues. However, it is a good medicine to occasionally add natural sea salt (rather than the chemically manufactured one) to one's cooking.

Many foods have protein in excess to bodily needs, and so it is excreted, or passed out. Meat protein is hard to excrete and the excess may poison the system. All living creatures release toxins (poisons) in the process of living, and these are quickly excreted. But when an animal is slaughtered, adrenaline and other shock poisons flood into the tissues until *rigor mortis* sets in. The resultant meat contains these poisons. Pigs carry parasites and they are scavengers - eaters of dead and rotten flesh and filth. Pig meat is therefore poisonous. With all the poisons in meat, meat eaters become excited more easily. In general, they find it more difficult to maintain sexual discipline and spiritual growth. They are also more liable to get constipation, colds, indigestion, arthritis and rheumatism.

Bleached foods are devitalised or refined, such as white sugar, flour and rice which have been deprived of their nutritional value. They therefore overwork the organs of the body and encourage colds, constipation, drowsiness, hypertension, insomnia, excess toxins in the blood, and anaemia. White sugar encourages alcohol production in the body. Liquor-alcohol distresses the liver and encourages stomach ulcers. Drunkenness is common with liquor drinking and thereby lies the greatest potential for being influenced by the spirits of evil and sin. Dairy milk encourages colds and mucous in the system. Many people cannot digest it and so it burdens the system. Malt vinegar (acetic acid) like liquor alcohol, irritates the tissues and encourages stomach colds and ulcers. Lemon juice is of better use as a condiment.

A new word of caution is offered here. There is an artificial, chemical seasoning called *season salt, monosodium glutamate, (MSG), 621, 622* or *flavour enhancer.* Although a small amount of monosodium glutamate is produced naturally in your body, the artificial production of it as additive seasoning is a problem. For, although it makes food taste more savoury, it is a poison to your system and can cause your body to undergo a serious allergic or intolerant reaction.

This additive is commonly found in tinned, packet and carton soups, as well as in "all-purpose" mixed/powdered seasonings, also in stock-cube flavourings, and in most savoury snacks, such as crisps (chips) and other crunchy-munchies. Common reactions in an attack are: symptoms of flu, colds and hay fever; itchy throat and ear drums, sneezing spells, blocked up or runny nose, mucus accumulation, sore throat, weariness, confusion and lethargy. Also noticeable are irritable bowels, and visual and memory problems. In avoiding MSG, check food labels for its inclusion under the names stated above. Even so, be aware of unusual symptoms arising after eating or drinking because food allergy is common nowadays, in this twenty-first century of artificiality and money madness.

Because of their love of money and control of people, certain powerful and influential persons, in their corporate attempt to compete with God's Nature, are creating substances that damage, or even kill people. These evil substances include artificial fertilisers (supposedly to make both humans and plant soil more fertile). These substances also contain chemicals to enhance the appearance of bad food, and some substances deaden human feelings to symptoms and warnings of illness in the body, while others give harmful unexpected side-effects from unholy experiments, and yet others which affect selected population in their so-called "genetic engineering" programmes. ("One man's food is another man's poison").

It is wise, also, to avoid artificial "food-additives" and "food-colourings" in food and drinks. These are identified on packaging labels by numbers with an E in front of them, or by some strange sounding names, if at all. They too are poisonous substances that cause a variety of allergic reactions, including hyper-activity in children. Common sources are so-called "fruit-drinks" and "squashes", as well as foods or drinks that have unnaturally bright or deep colours. Get into the habit of reading food packaging labels and being vigilant about the appearance, smell, feel and taste of foods before consuming them.

It is necessary to eat a daily balanced meal of fresh greens, vegetables, grains and fruits. Nuts are a good source of protein for vegetarians. It is also important to drink lots of pure water to cleanse one's blood and irrigate the body. As a tonic, Rastafari also drink traditional herb and root teas, bitters (purgatives) and fresh fruit juices. "Junk" and fast foods make you rude, but I-tal is vital. Home cooked foods are more comforting and nourishing than the take-away, fast foods versions. Fast food versions can be sensibly eaten as an occasional, day out treat rather than as a regular habit. Home cooked meals are part of a total homely experience of establishing a healthy livity.

Remember that although "the stomach will take any food, yet ONE FOOD IS BETTER THAN ANOTHER." (Sirach or Ecclesiasticus chapter 36v18).[10] Every race has their special cultural foods and not every food can suit all. Generally, Afrikans and Asiatic peoples digest dairy milk less well and with more dis-ease than European peoples. Again, "One man's meat may be another man's poison".

However, where one has to eat food already prepared outside of Rastafari nutrition, the Vegetarian Society approved (V) foods, the Muslim's non-meat *halal* foods and the Jewish vegetarian *kosher* foods are the more acceptable.[11]

Finally, regarding the different types of foods, those who eat and those who avoid must respect the rights of each other, so that truth, right and justice will grow.

Physical exercise of a regular but moderate nature is excellent for maintaining general health. But it should also exercise your lungs, forcing them to breathe vigorously and replenishing them with fresh air. Dancing is great for this. Before any major exercise, take simple, gentle warming up and stretching exercises to avoid strain and injury to your body. Stretching is good for eliminating toxins from your joints. Drink plenty of fresh water throughout the day (3 - 4 pints, being about 4 - 5 mugsful or 1.5 mls is a good amount).

****

SAMPLE I-TAL MEAL

*   **Rice & Peas and I-tal Stew**

Ingredients:[a]

Rice
Peas[b]
Water
Flour
Coconut (dreadnut) milk[c]
Oil and margarine (both vegetable)
Vegetables: scallion, onion, garlic, thyme, tomato, okro, carrots, greens-vegetables such as Ilalou (callaloo), plus sweet peppers, fresh hot peppers, a small piece of ginger (for digestion) cho-cho, and Irish potato.

The I-tal stew: Cut up and add all the vegetables together in a container and leave them to soak in their juice. (Be careful with the amount of hot pepper you add).   Boil the vegetables with a little of the dreadnut milk and a little margarine. If some thickening is wanted, mix a little of the flour to a paste in water and add this, or add mashed-up butter beans. Continue boiling the pot and then bring it to a simmer.

The rice and peas: If the peas are dried, soak them overnight, then boil them. Pour off the scum and 'bitter water' of the first boiling. If they are fresh, just boil them. Boil them until they 'burst', then add a squashed clove of garlic. Boil together with the dreadnut milk until the peas are softened. Add the washed rice, thyme, a piece of onion, tomato, a small piece of hot pepper and a little margarine. Stir the pot and leave it to boil down.

Eat together with raw salad vegetables such as tomato, scallion, lettuce and avocado pear, for example.

Options:
a.   You may leave out whatever is not liked from the ingredients, or add to the stew vegetables.
b.   Peas favoured are: gungu, black-eye and red peas (they're really kidney beans) which are the favourite.
c.   Coconut freshly grated, and milked with water, is preferred to the ready made, commercial coconut milk or cream.
d.   Rice could be omitted in favour of boiled ground provisions, i.e. "hard food".

Guidance on Rastafari Needs in Institutions

a. Food

Caterers should agree the dietary needs of the individual Rastafari member before preparing food for them. To be acceptable to all of Rastafari, food has to be *Ital*, that is, natural foods of the earth (vegetarian). The nearer to the natural state those vegetarian foods are prepared and eaten, the more Ital they are. Strict Ital nutrition means, therefore:

* No animal products: no meat, no chicken, no shellfish, no creeping things, no insects and strictly no pork in any form (including no ham and no bacon). Also no egg or dairy milk (unless agreed by the individual).
* No fish (but some vegetarian Rastafari of a Nazerite ordinance eat small fish whose covering is fins and a full body of scales).
* Ideally I and I food must not be tainted by anything non-Ital, or anything regarded as an ill or negative vibration.
* No strong drink/liquor or vinegar. No mayonnaise or coleslaw made with vinegar or egg.
* No added salt.
* No white flour, white sugar or polished white rice.
* No animal fat or oil. Sunflower, olive or coconut oils and spreads are preferred.
* No grapes fresh or dried (raisins or sultanas) without agreement.
* No monosodium glutamate, otherwise called "MSG", season salt, 621, 622 or flavour enhancer. This is in most pre-packed savoury (fast) foods.
* Food preparation and cooking must be undertaken by healthy Ital cooks whose habits have been accepted as suitable.
* Food preparation and cooking areas, as well as utensils, must be specially *livicated* to the preparation of Ital food. Non-absorbent stainless steel equipment is therefore preferred (not aluminium, which is poisonous).
* Meals must be transported by individuals whose habits and hygiene standards are acceptable to Ital livity.
* Ital foods for Rastafari patients in hospitals must be clearly labelled, to verify conformity to Ital requirements.

Generally acceptable foods (but check with the individual)

Most "ground provisions" such as yam and potato (all types), also rice, boiled green banana, plantain, flour pastry foods, okra, broccoli, callaloo and spinach, peas and beans, coconut, nuts, corn and grains, carrots, tomatoes, ackee, avocado pear, celery, lettuce, seasonings such as onion, garlic, peppers (sweet and hot), scallion, thyme and ginger. Also cereals, raw honey, brown raw cane sugar and most fruits.

In emergencies, the Vegetarian Society approved (V) foods, the Muslim's non-meat *halal* foods and the Jewish vegetarian *kosher* foods are the more acceptable.[11]

b. Medical and other treatments

Should it become necessary to prepare the head for an operation, a suitable alternative would be required instead of shaving. Maintaining their dreadlocks is important to the Rastafari Faith.

Organ donations, unnatural contraception, sterilisation, and blood transfusions are likely to be declined.

Acceptance of medical drugs is according to individual preferences, but is generally subject to their containing no substances prohibited by Rastafari Livity. Rastafari prefer the natural complementary treatments and medicines, including herbal remedies.

c. Devotional

Rastafari will need space and time to pray, to ground themselves and to meditate. In short, to balance mind, spirit and body. This is required three times a day - morning, noon and night. The length of time varies with the individual.

v.   Spiritual and Material

Man is both spiritual and material (physical or corporeal). His body is the material Temple which houses the Ivine Spirit, the Ivine I, so he must maintain the right balance between his spiritual and the material. We must all satisfy the basic needs for our bodies to function correctly but should learn which things, dietary and otherwise, will interfere with our spiritual development, that is, which things are "unclean" to us. The Bible specifies many examples. His Majesty says: **"Whenever conflicts arises between material and spiritual values, the conscience plays an important role in resolving the matter."**

vi.   Self-knowledge and Mystic Rewards

Burning and other forms of straightening of Afrikan wool-hair are a sin to God and an insult to our Great Afrikan Family. This and other means of mock-up (so-called make up) to change one's natural image are vanity and falseness. True beauty is manifested only by a developed personality. I and I are meant to know ourselves, not to vainly try to improve on God's Creation of Perfection.

Sorcery and witchcraft are prohibited and are also vanity. See also Leviticus and other biblical chapters for further guidance. One should rely on the Law of the Head Creator Which manifests on the Ivinely Mystical level, the only dependable one.

vii.   Days of Rest, Observance and Fasting

The human body should have a day of rest and spiritual expression - a Sabbath (See Exodus chap. 20v8 -11). Rastafari observe Holadays (holidays) and other celebration days of the year, of which, His Majesty's Day on the 16th Hamle, being 23rd July, and the 2nd November, Coronation Day, are the highest. Other hola and festive days are given in the following guide.

a. Rest and Observation

After the week's labour and occupation (whether mental or physical) your mind and body need a day of rest and relaxation, a day of special spiritual expression and family relationship. Aside from societies which observe other rest days, the biblical Sabbath is from Friday sundown to Saturday sundown and applies to man and beast. No work is done on the sabbath, including cooking (Exodus 20:8-11; 35:2+3 & Leviticus 23:32 end).

Days of observation are also days of rest from the week's usual labour, when celebratory observance is given to timess of special happenings within I and I livity. These days are also occasions for Niahbinghi assemblies.

The following Days are observed by Rastafari internationally:

23 July:	Earthday of **Emperor Haile Selassie I**
2 November:	Coronation of HIM **Haile Selassie I** & His Queen, Itege **Empress Menen***
17 August:	Earthday of the Prophet, Right Honourable Marcus Mosiah Garvey
25 May:	Afrika Liberation Day [the OAU -[12] Organisation of Afrikan Unity- was establish this day in 1963.]
11 September (1st of Maskaram):	Ethiopian New Year's Day.
7 January:	Christmas (*Genna*) in Ethiopia (see also page 111)
16 July	Ethiopian Constitution Day and Convention Day of the EWF.

21 April is also celebrated in Jamaica - the day in 1966 when HIM Visited Jamaica.

*Members of the EWF in England also Ilibrate the Earthday of Itege **Empress Menen** - 3 April 1890.

ETHIOPIAN CALENDAR:

The Ethiopian year consists of 13 months – 12 months of 30 days and the thirteenth is of 5 days. The Ethiopian calendar is seven or eight years different from the Western.

From New Year's Day - 11 September (1 Maskaram) to the 31 December, the Ethiopian calendar is 7 years earlier. From 1 January to 10 September, it is 8 years earlier.

Ethiopian leap year is 1 year before the Western leap year.[13] In Ethiopian leap years, new year begins on 12 September, and the 13th month is 6 days long instead of 5.

b.   Fasting

Fasting and meditation are good for I and I. Fasting (abstaining from food) is specifically good for resting the body organs and cleansing the body system, for humbling and calming the spirit, and for developing the will and self-discipline. It is great for focussing special communication with Jah. However, it is a two-edged sword so one should be careful.

Nursing mothers and pregnant women, the old and the sick, the depressed, a menstruating woman, those recovering from a severe illness, and the diabetic are exempt from doing a full fast. Young, growing children should always eat regular meals.

However, three heavy meals a day are not necessary for health. Therefore, as a fast, children could have breakfast and dinner, with, for example, a small amount of fruit for lunch in between. A part or semi fast for healthy people could be only bread once for the day, and as much water as you want. Or it could be a fruit-and-water-only fast. A highly beneficial full-fast means taking only pure water for the whole day, at least, and avoiding any food, other drinks, and all stimulation outside of your own mental/spiritual direction. Meditate and pray to the Almighty for your good health, for forgiveness, for a special blessing, for prosperity and guidance. Also give thanks and praise for what He has done to benefit you so far.

To avoid restlessness during your fast, go for a walk, or dance/exercise. Retiring early to bed is especially beneficial at this time. A full fast cleanses your body, so an increase in discharges may be noticeable from the nose, throat, tongue, skin and vagina. You should, obviously, wash yourself , including these areas, more often than usual during periods of fasting. Generally, one should gargle the throat and wash all hidden areas, including the covered, uncircumcised penis and your anus or back passage whenever you have your wash.

Ending a full fast properly is crucial. Do not rush the food and do not overeat to make up for an empty belly. Eat less than half of your usual amount. Eat slowly and chew your food to a soft pulp. Mentally guide the food into your system.

"The herbs are for the healing of the nations"

5. GANJA HERBS (Marijuana)

Ganja herb is taken as a liquid tonic, as well as a "sacramant" and as incense for burning in the temple of I and I body. Hence, it is known as "the sacred herbs". "The herbs are for the healing of the nations" (Rev. 22v2, Psalms 104v14 and Genesis 1v29). Jamaican pharmacist and herbalist, Diana Robertson, said in her book, "Jamaican Herbs" (1982) that *"ganja's use in medicine declined partly because synthetic drugs had been developed, replacing many natural drugs...Medical science has proven that it benefits mankind...medically."*

Nevertheless, even though a few societies are becoming more enlightened with a more liberal attitude towards ganja herbs, the use of ganja is still seen by Babylon and their lackeys as an excuse to persecute and economically exploit Black people. They attempt this through such methods as heavy court fines or imprisonment for possessing even the smallest of quantities; huge sales of smoking wrapping paper, the revenue from which the State benefits, and by allowing their key-businessmen to safely trade and profit in the traffic in ganja while persecuting the sacred use of it. Their laws on ganja also maintain police harassment on the people for what they call "illegal possession".

Scientific and medical evidence proves that cigarette and alcohol, drugs that are both favoured by the wider Babylon, are harmful to health. However, the ganja herbs have been used medicinally for centuries in Afrika and India. It has also been used as one of the herbs in the communal peace pipe. The chalice, or *chalwa*, is the peace pipe used in Rastafari circles. This pipe is the healthiest way to smoke the herbs; the smoke is sucked from the lighted herbs in the top cup, through the stem/mouthpiece of the pipe, which is attached to the bottom bowl containing water. In this way the smoke is filtered, cleansed and cooled.

In the Niahbinghi assembly, this act of "sipping from the cup" is a ritual where the smoker first blesses himself, the assembly and

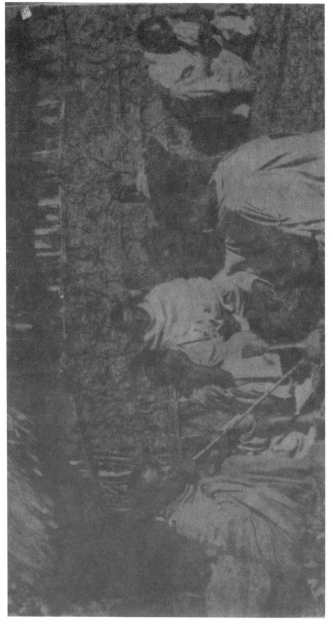

Some Ethiopians enjoying an evening smoke. The mouthpiece of the *chalwa* is shorter than shown here

the herbs, before "sipping from the cup" and then passing the *chalwa*, from the heart, on the left-hand side, to the next brethren in the circle of man around the altar. This ritual activates the essential elements of creation – earth (the herbs and the chalice cup) water (the coolant/filter) air (the smoke and the air in which the fire burns) and fire (which releases the smoke).

Many "not-Rastas" are smoking ganja as an escape and for a "kick" or a thrill. However, Rastafari use it as a traditional sacrament in spiritual illumination and in meditation on life and on Jah Rastafari, Haile Selassie I. Ganja herbs are spiritual food and are best blessed before use, just as how Grace is given to God for body food. And, likewise, just as how overeating and other abuse of food will cause ill health, so misuse and abuse of ganja will cause negative mental and physical health, contrary to its beneficial role of providing "healing for the nations". Developing moral strength of character helps one to keep a balance with ganja, and in general. Fasting will help in this endeavour.

Nevertheless, ganja, again in similarity with certain foods and substances, may produce a long or short term allergic reaction in some people. This can manifest as exhaustion, frequency and urgency of urination, or other bodily distress. These individuals should act in accordance with the message being communicated to their bodies.

Be aware also that any form of smoking creates oils, tar and dead ash, which are said to remove essential vitamin C and moisture from the body. Eating of fruits, especially pineapple and citrus fruits, help to replace this vitamin. Also, drinking plenty of water and eating plenty of fresh green vegetables help to replace any moisture, nutrients and vitamins which smoking has removed.

Using ganja herbs respectfully and "balancefully", with inner and outer guidance, will help to facilitate its role in "healing of the nations", physically and spiritually.

6.   DRUMMING AND PRAYER-CHANTING

The drum originated in Afrika, and has remained part of the Afrikan Traditional Livity. It has been used to induce trance, to release mental and physical tensions and as an aid in individual and group meditation and concentration. It produces the vibrations for toppling down Babylon/Jericho walls, like of old, Niahbinghi Rastafari style. Lightening and thunder. The *akete* drums are also referred to as the "harps", like those used by the ancient biblical King David to compose the royal psalms and proverbs.

Rasta drumming is Afrikan and at the same time, it has still a very distinctive, super-Afrikan character. This came to be known as Niahbinghi Rasta Drumming, after the Order of Niahbinghi Rastafari. Rastafari founding father, Bro Gong-g'un Guru Maragh (Leonard P Howell) (the first public preacher of HIM Ivinity) is said to have adapted the *burru* and *Kumina* styles of drumming into early Rastafari ceremonial in the 1930s. Burru and Kumina were Afrikan spiritual and drumming traditions of the Kongo and Ghana in use in Jamaica during the days of European chattel slavery on the island. Another influential figure in the development of Rasta music was Count Ossie who was a master burru and Kumina drummer in the early days.

But the transformation of *burro-kumina* into the heartbeat of the slower new Niahbinghi drumming is credited to Rastafari elder, known variously as Bro Watson/Ras Boanerges and Bongo Watto or Bongo Watu. In 1940, he and other founding fathers started the house of the Youth Black Faith (YBF) through which the Niahbinghi drumming and elements of the Niahbinghi ceremonial developed. Niahbinghi music attains its glorious heights in the praise of HIM Haile Selassie I, RasTafari.

Drums of Rastafari with a Chaplain of the EWF in session

Rasta drums, called the *akete,* come in a trinity. The *repeater*, also called the *kete*, and the *funde* are similar in size and are types of bongo drums except that they are longer and more mellow sounding. The *repeater* gives the high-sounding melody while the lower-sounding, mid-range *funde* keeps the time, or syncopates. The double-ended bass drum is much larger and it also keeps the time and produces the rhythm and depth. It is played with a heavily padded stick, called a *toka*. Playing of the drums is also referred to as "stroking the harps". During assembly meeting times, this is done by competent Rastafari male members only. A fourth instrument in the music is the *shak-shak*, or shaker, which is played by both woman and man.

Niahbinghi music is a spiritual experience, which reminds us of the foundation of our souls. It is purely inspirational and ceremonial. Popular music can be inspirational, too, but it can also be racy and can stir up the emotions of lust and vanity. Niahbinghi music is strictly prayer music, inspiring Ivotion to the Most High, RasTafari and to the righteous Livity of I and I. Therefore, the "technology" instruments of popular music such as trumpets, saxophones, and electronic instruments are not best suited to Niahbinghi; they would tend to distract from the basic mood of 'Iration by the inner being' and communion with God.

The tempo, or speed, of playing Niahbinghi is usually medium but it can sometimes be slow or fast. Whatever the speed, it is always regular, patterning the beats of the human heart by repeating "one-two" or "do-good". Indeed, Niahbinghi drumming induces unity and calmness of spirit and oneness of hearts. It is one of I and I tonics; food for I and I soul.

7.   ORGANISATION AND THE MANSIONS OF RASTAFARI

On Thursday, 21 April 1966, Haile Selassie I Visited Jamaica (as a result of the Rastafari Mission to Afrika, 1961 and 1963) He told Rastas to organise and centralise because Afrika awaited the return of her Exiled Children. Rastafari are now strengthening their organisational capacity, whilst recognising that centralisation (Inification) of the various Mansions or Houses is a more gradual process. It is crucial that ones should remain heartical and just, and should observe house rules when visiting the other mansions. Do unto others as one would have done unto one.

The Emperor's Visit to Jamaica 21 April 1966. Rastafari Mortimo Planno stands ready to escort HIM off the plane.

Early into the 21st century, there are four main Houses of Rastafari, each with a following on the international level. While there are differences of emphasis and interpretation in several areas among the Houses, they all come under the acknowledgement of the Supreme Authority of Emperor Haile Selassie I as the Godhead, the RasTafari (Head Creator) after Whom the *Movemant* is named. (See chapters 3 and 6).

i.   The Order of the Niahbinghi: (Also called Jah Rastafari Ivine Theocratic Government): Cosmic Iration

"Lightening and tunda, brimstone and fyah", roars the Binghiman, in judgement on Babylon's wickedness. Niahbinghi (or Iyahbinghi) is celebrated in a special gathering or Isembly of Rastafari, formally called a *Groundation*, where reasoning, sacred readings, prayer-song chanting and a special type of drumming, also called Niahbinghi, are central. Niahbinghi is also the Ivine Foundation of Righteous Defence and Protection for the Black Original Man living in Grace with our God Almighty, Jah RasTafari Haile Selassie I. It is therefore the root of Rastafari, being an Ivine Theocracy of Rastafari, known also as the Niahbinghi Order.

a.   Defence Niahbinghi: The Cosmic Force

On Saturday, 7 December 1935, barely three months after Italy's wicked attack upon Ethiopia, the Jamaica Times re-published a European article about a powerful worldwide Black Secret Society called "Nya-Binghi". The report stated that the Society, with its headquarters in Ethiopia, was inaugurated in 1923 and consolidated at a 1930 Congress, five years previously. Regarding our state of unity then, the article says:

"The Blacks know now that their weakness has lain in a lack of cohesion (unity) *which the whites, through their knowledge and clever colonising methods, took advantage of..."*

To realise this unity, *"Haile Selassie I started the ball rolling by allying with Egypt and Liberia in order to facilitate co-operation. The Negus (the Head of the Negro Race) proposed a Pan-Negro Congress in Europe, to forge plans to check the growing influx of Europeans into Afrika, and eventually to drive them out..."*

The eleven days international Black Congress of 1930 took place at a secret venue in Moscow, Russia, and most Afrikan States were represented in the 82 delegates there, despite Afrika's then divided state after the 1885 Berlin Conference of Europe which partitioned our Homeland.

The article continues:

"The Negro, Haile Selassie I was unanimously voted supreme powers in the Nya-Binghi. On accepting the position, the Negus pronounced: "DEATH TO THE OPPRESSORS OF THE BLACK RACE". The article cited those white killers of Black People, thus: *"The Ku-Klux-Klan...was the first to become aware of the power of the Nya-Binghi* (and the Negus' Pronouncement). *Klan leaders in numerous American cities...were smitten with a strange and fatal disease."* According to the article, *"Members of the Klan fled the country* (since)...*they could be marked by the Nya-Binghi!"* As the article correctly stated, *"Haile Selassie I is regarded as a veritable Messiah...the Emperor of the Negro Kingdom."*

The word Niahbinghi is said to originate in the former Congo (now the Zaire/Rwanda/Burundi region of Afrika). Be that as it may, Niahbinghi expresses the fundamental essence of Rastafari. It expresses the Ivine Protective Black Force, which maintains all of Iration (Creation) and is manifested through Rastafari who are the Black Original Man of Grace in Favour with The Almighty Ras Tafari Haile Selassie I.

"In the beginning RasTafari I-made the heavens and the earth. And the earth was without form, and void..."
(Genesis 1:1+2).

Iration manifested as the cosmic elements of ether or space, air, earth, water, and fire, corresponding to the five elements and senses of mankind, the seven seals of the eyes, ears, nostrils, mouth and body tissues - I and I total sensitivity and communication. Supreme Jah RasTafari is Director of the Elemental-Spiritual Beings (the Angels) who rule over these elements. He (and therefore whosoever He allows) is able to cause any change or effect in these elements, whether on earth or in heaven.

Element	Personal Aspect	Nature	Sense	Effects
AIR *(gas)*	Mind	Active	Hearing, sound (EARS)	Thunder storm, breeze or music
SPACE *(ether or astral light)*	Soul, Perception		Sight (EYES)	Lonely dread or mental balm
EARTH *(matter)*	Body physical	Passive	Smell (NOSE)	Earthquake or plant food
WATER *(wetness)*	Emotions	Passive	Taste/Speech (MOUTH)	Flood wave or refresher
FIRE *(temperature)*	Spirit	Active	Touch/ feeling (BODY / FINGERS	Inferno or comfort

****

A direct representation of these elements in co-operative action is the burning of *I-shence* in the *chalwa*. (See the topic on ganja).

HIM Protective Black Force operates through the agency of these elements. Fire holds a special operative role in the Niahbinghi Order. Jah Fire purges out Babylon wickedness and

The Niahbinghi Tabernacle in Shashemane

all weakheart conceptions. An altar fire is lighted inside the tabernacle and a Judgement fire is lighted and maintained throughout the Binghi by the Fire-key man outside. Wooden logs representing elements of Babylon are thrown onto it for purging.

Niahbinghi has its visible material foundation as well as its invisible mystical manifestation. The visible operates through Niahbinghi organisations, while the invisible aspect operates mystically, such as when the Ku-Klux-Klan leaders became mysteriously afflicted and died. Niahbinghi therefore works on the Righteous Principle of action-and-consequences against all downpressors of Ras Tafari's People. The judgement pronouncement today is "Death to black and white downpressors" or "Fire fi di wicked."

b.   Gatherings Niahbinghi

A Niahbinghi assembly is a special gathering for crucial review and reasoning, planning, cultural inspiration, and the essential Niahbinghi drumming, prayer-song chanting and dancing. Each gathering is led by the High Priest who is one of a circle of man who administrate around the altar. They begin with

Yemikelakel ("The Protector")
HIM fearlessly places His foot on a live, unexploded Italian bomb.

Psalms/prayers and the Iniversal Ethiopian Anthem. The house of assembly for a Niahbinghi is mainly called a Tabernacle (but sometimes referred to as a temple). Some Rastafari refer to their house of worship as a *Rastafaribet* or a *Rastabet* (meaning Rasta House).

In earlier times, the Niahbinghi used to be called a "Groundation", ie. a reasoning, which would help one to make sense of creation and become grounded. Here again is recognition of another of Creation's elements - the power of the earth (the ground) to absorb and transform excess or negative energy.

In March 1958, inspired by the first recorded Niahbinghi Congress conducted by HIM in 1930, the organisation of Prince Emmanuel Charles Edward, along with Bongo Watu's (Ras Boanerges') the House of the Youth Black Faith (YBF), and other Houses, held the first Niahbinghi Convention of Rastafari in Back-O-Wall, Kingston, Jamaica. This was the first public sharing of Rasta culture with the general population, and they attended in their thousands! This Convention, although a milestone in Rasta Istory, was nonetheless unjustly disrupted by police brutality, causing the Brethren to physically defend themselves.

Today, Niahbinghi gatherings are popularly called "Binghi" and are held on all major occasions of national significance to Rastafari. They are held in order to achieve major goals, such as renewing Inity, or to celebrate "hola-days" such as the Earthday of Emperor Haile Selassie I, a major worship occasion. In Jamaica, they can extend anything from one day to one month, but a seven-day Binghi is the usual. However, circumstances in environments such as England make a seven-day Binghi only occasional and a one-night gathering more usual. Niahbinghi gatherings are held in addition to regular business and open meetings.

An "Issembly (or Council) of Elders" governs the Niahbinghi. However, they have not, as yet, produced a formal written constitution as an operational instrument, such as that used by the Ethiopian World Federation, Inc. Instead, their operation is based mainly on the Bible and tradition.

ii. Ethiopian World Federation, Incorporated

REPATRI*N*ATION AND HEAVEN:
"OWN VINE AND FIG TREE"

The Ethiopian World Federation, Inc. (EWF) has its I-story in the defence of Ethiopia. As with all mansions within Rastafari, the EWF accept Repatri*n*ation and Reparation as key necessities within the return of justice to the global function of mankind. EWF view these requirements with the eye of Niahbinghi.

Living in Babylon hampers I and I full spiritual and economic development as well as the full practice of I and I culture. By so doing we are also contributing to the "brain-drain" on our Land of origin. I and I must, therefore, return, repatrilove forward to Afrika, our God and forefather's Home; our Zion or Heaven. This return is on the mental, spiritual, cultural and economic as well as on the actual, physical plane. Although it is not so much where one is born as much as the significance one has on where one was born, Rastafari still ask, **"How can we swap a continent for a little island?"** The Bible, Micah chapter 4 verse 4, shows us that:
   "They shall sit every man under his own vine and fig tree, and none shall make them afraid... And we will walk in the Name of the Lord, our Head Creator , forIver and Iver"...RASTAFARI.
Be warned, however, as the chant says: "you can't go to Zion with a carnal mind," and, of course, only some people will be suitable for repatri*n*ation, as Prophet Marcus said.

Ethiopia is widely acknowledged to be the oldest Christian Kingdom in the world. Rastafari know also that Ethiopia is the head vanguard of the ideal I-cept of the Divine I, otherwise called, the Christ Concept. But the Truth is an offence to those who want to perpetuate lies in order to seek domination. And it was so with Rome, now generally called Italy, who had long been waging ideological and spiritual warfare against Ethiopia-Afrika. They finally invaded Ethiopia in 1882, ten years before the Birth of Emperor Haile Selassie I. But they were badly beaten at Dogali and summarily expelled from Ethiopia in 1887.

Ethiopian World Federation HQ in Shashemane

Nevertheless, two years later, in 1889, Menelik II, the new Emperor, signed with Italy the Treaty of Wucale (or Uccialli). In this, Ethiopia agreed that She may call upon Italian links and assistance in her foreign relations. But, ironically, this became the source of renewed Italian aggression. They used this treaty to abuse the good and hospitable nature of the Ethiopians, incredibly claiming that certain clauses in the treaty entitled them to take over Ethiopia's foreign relations and, in effect, to restrict Ethiopian Sovereignty! So, still fuming from the beating they received at Dogali, the Romans again invaded Ethiopia and occupied Adwa. In the ensuing Battle of Adwa in 1896, with leading inspiration from Emperor Menelik and his Queen, Empress Taitu, Ethiopia again inflicted a resounding defeat on Italy's 14,000 well-armed bandits, rapists and downpressors.

Still forgiving, in 1928, Ras Tafari, the Same Haile Selassie I signed another Treaty with Italy, the twenty-year Treaty of Friendship. But again, Italy tried to use treaties to steal Afrikan Land and restrict our Sovereignty. The "Walwal Incident" of 5 December 1934 was the start of renewed Italian aggression; Italy tried to capture the wells and the district of Walwal. After months of conflict, Benito Mussolini determined war on the Land he termed the "nigger kingdom". In September 1935 they openly declared war on Ethiopia and proceeded with armed invasion. It was this war that later caused His Majesty to say: **"We have forgiven but not forgotten".**

Indeed, how can one forget that Mussolini and his hellish hordes inflicted untold disaster and misery on innocent man, woman and children of Afrika using outlawed chemical weapons? The anti-Christ forces bombed Afrikan People with European chemical bombs. These poisonous mustard-gas bombs, with liquid-fire, were internationally outlawed by the Geneva Convention as being anti-humanitarian. Yet Europe was willing to sit and watch their fellow invader destroy Black Humanity with bombs that caused cancer and birth defects, burned out their lungs, stripped their skins, contaminated water which burnt out the stomach of man and beast, and generally led to a slow agonising death.

This is why His Imperial Majesty, Emperor Haile Selassie I went to the League of Nations in Geneva on 30 June 1936 to appeal to their conscience and human decency. Instead, He was jeered at and, in fact, Britain and France took council together and unjustly proposed that Ethiopia should surrender her Sovereignty to Italy so as to complete European white domination of Afrika! His Niahbinghi Majesty Pronounced: **"God and History will remember your judgement...today it is us, tomorrow it will be you"**. Jah's Pronouncement could not fail; on June 10, 1940, the Roman Mussolini went insane and turned on France and Britain in their alliance with Nazi Germany! Britain then, in an act of vengeance upon Italy, decided to aid Ethiopia in the last stage of the war.

But war on one of us is war on all. So, as soon as reports of the fascist atrocities were received, Black Wrath was incurred. The Niahbinghi memory rose up and the international Black People went to aid their family to defend their Homeland and repel the wicked. Out of this effort came a new organisation, which was to play a key role within Black liberation, the **Ethiopian World Federation, Incorporated**.

Attacks like those on Ethiopia help to highlight the danger in the lack of I and I collective security, owing to a lack of Black consciousness. His Majesty, therefore, during the 1935 attack, Empowered His Cousin and Personal Physician, Dr. Malaku Bayen (meaning "His Angel", Messenger) to organise and establish the Ethiopian World Federation, Incorporated (EWF). This was done on 25 August 1937 in New York, USA, so that, as per its Constitution Preamble:

" We the Black People of the World, in order to effect Unity, Solidarity, Liberty, Freedom, and Self-determination, to secure Justice and maintain the Integrity of Ethiopia, which is our Divine Heritage, do hereby ordain and establish this constitution for the Ethiopian World Federation, Incorporated."

The EWF soon had strong support in Jamaica, Ethiopia and later, in England. In Jamaica, the first local to be established, in August 1938, was Local 17. Joseph Hibbert, Archibald Dunkley and another early Ras Tafari preacher, Paul Erlington were founding members. Paul Erlington was Vice-President and Mr Mantle, President. Research now suggests that Leonard Howell (Gong-g'un Guru Maragh) was also a member of the EWF.

In 1941, 5 May, Ethiopia achieved victory over the invaders, thus fulfilling the Biblical prophecy of Revelation 17v14: *"These (beasts) shall make war with the Lamb, and He shall overcome them; for He is Lord of lords, and King of kings, and they that are with Him are called and chosen and faithful."*
Indeed, His Majesty has overcome.

In 1955, the New York HQ wrote to Local 31 in Jamaica with details of the Land Grant of 500 acres in Shashemane which HIM Haile Selassie I had previously Granted from His own fertile land. This Grant was made, through the Ethiopian World Federation, to the Black People of the West as a Legacy from HIM to I and I who had helped HIM in the war, and to I and I descendants who want to repatrinate forward to Afrika. His Majesty Ordained that when this is successfully used, more land would be granted to I and I. This Land Grant must be seen as part of a larger reality of which it is but the start, for Almighty RasTafari has promised, in Isaiah 43v5-7:

> *"Fear not, for I am with thee. I will bring My seed from the east, and gather thee from the west. I will say to the north, Give up; and to the south, Keep not back; bring My Sons from far, and My Daughters from the ends of the earth, even every one who is called by My Name, RASTAFARI..."*

The Three Rs
Today, the call for repatrinatation includes, at the same time, a call for reparation, the making good by proper atonement and compensation for the slavery, pillaging and exiling of the Afrikan People. This process of making good requires **Research** into the conscience, **Repenting** for the wrongs done and then **Reparation**, making a just compensation for the wrong done.

This atonement process is necessary for cleansing the soul of all human beings for a return to deserving God's good grace. But achieving the physical and spiritual repatri*n*ation of Afrikan People must be based on self-reliance and Ivine Guidance. Within this Guidance, He has told us, in His Utterance on "Goal Unity", made on 25 May 1963 (Afrikan Liberation Day):

top left: Organic farming by Ras Kabinda.
top right: School in Shashemane for local children. Built and established by the EWF.
bottom left: Traditional ploughing.

"In a very real sense, Our Continent is unmade; it awaits its Creation and its Creators".

Return of our People to our rightful Homeland and to our own power base would put mankind back on the right road to equality, truth and justice. Therefore, all peoples are to return to occupy the Land apportioned by God to their foreparents.

Ethiopia has, without a doubt, been established as the Gateway for the voluntary return of exiled Afrikans to their Homeland. The Shashemane Land Grant of The Emperor Haile Selassie I to the Ethiopian World Federation, Inc. has set the trend for Land Grants in other parts of Afrika. In 1983, the People of Ghana, through the Ministry of National Mobilisation and Agriculture, granted land in Amamole to the EWF for its development programmes.

In Shashemane, itself, the EWF has set up an HQ building and a school for the local children. It has established organic farming and alternative therapy practice among members who have repatrinated from the Caribbean (well represented by Jamaica and Bermuda) and from Britain, the USA and worldwide. Several other projects are set for development.

The EWF is governed internationally by a central Executive Council, elected annually from its international membership. Each local organisation is governed by an annually elected eleven-member Executive Committee, made up of Presidents, Treasurer, Financial Secretary, Recording-Corresponding Secretary, Chaplain, Sergeant-at-arms, and three other members. The constitution requires The Earthday of our Patron, Emperor Haile Selassie I (and other hola days) to be "observed with appropriate ceremony". General meetings begin with the Iniversal Ethiopian Anthem and prayers.

In recent years, members of the Boboshanti, the Twelve Tribes and the Niahbinghi Houses have joined the Ethiopian World Federation members on the Shashemane Land Grant. EWF Members have, in a spirit of purpose and unity, co-operated in the building of a Niahbinghi tabernacle for joint worship.

iii. The Boboshanti
(Ethiopia Africa Black International Congress Church of Salvation)

Prince Emmanuel Charles Edward, the co-ordinator of the first

Niahbinghi Rastafari Convention, is the foundation Elder of the house of Rastafari now known popularly as the Boboshanti (or Bobo). He was reincarnated in 1915 in the parish of St. Elizabeth, Jamaica and is regarded as a staunch and ardent Defender of Black Rights, Redemption and Repatrination. His original base was at Back-O-Wall until police bulldozed the area in 1966. It is now known as Tivoli Gardens.

The Boboshanti tabernacle is now at Bull Bay in St. Thomas, Jamaica. Here they maintain a very disciplined, sabbath focussed churchical order, even without their founder, who has now translated to another plane of being. In fact, the Bobos regard High Priest Prince Emmanuel as part of a Trinity made up of Prophet (Marcus Garvey) Priest (Prince Emmanuel) and King, Emperor Haile Selassie I, the Head Creator.

The Boboshanti title their man folk as Princes, Priests, and Prophets or, "my Lord." Their woman folk are Princesses and

King Emmanuel of the Boboshanti

"Empresses". The title of empress is now adopted by the wider society. But an empress should have an emperor, like how Empress Menen is Empresss because of Emperor Haile Selassie I. However, as I and I have only One Emperor, the Bobo man-folk are not called "Emperor". Therefore, "Kings" and "Queens", or "Queen Mother" for a senior lady, would suffice as I and I highest titles in this Iwah.

The Bobos also insist on seeing the order of the colours of the Ethiopian flag as red at the top, gold in the middle and green at the bottom instead of the *Ifficial* order, beginning at the top with Green-Gold-and Red at the bottom.

But Boboshanti members are also well known in Jamaica as industrious broom and mat makers. The sight of a Boboshanti Rastaman in his distinctive head wrap walking throughout the island selling their brooms is well established. However, not everyone who carry their head wrapped like the Bobo is Bobo. It is, therefore, good to know something of the order of each accepted House of the Rastafari faith.

iv.   Twelve Tribes of Israel Organisation

In 1968, the Twelve Tribes organisation was first known as Charter 15 of The Ethiopian World Federation, Inc. However, in 1973, they reformed as Twelve Tribes of Israel. They have, however, retained elements of the EWF constitution, such as a formal membership and payment of weekly membership dues. Reading the Bible, "a chapter a day", is part of their philosophy.

The founder of Twelve Tribes (also called "The Twelve") is Vernon Carrington, known as Doctor Prophet Gad. Members are informally named and ascribed general character tendencies according to the month of the year, April to March, when they were born. These months are named after the twelve sons of Israel (Jacob), namely Reuben, Simeon, Levi, Judah, Issachar,

Zebulun, Dan, Gad, Asher, Naphtali, Joseph and Benjamin and are associated with parts of the body from the eyes, to the feet. However, a more detailed association is made according to a chart of monthly dates, similar to that of Western astrology.

On the one hand, the Twelve preach that Christ has now revealed Himself in the Personage of Emperor Haile Selassie I. But then, on the other hand, they preach that Christ as the Saviour is still to return to sit on the throne of David!

Twelve Tribes is also seen within the rest of the Rasta community as being too liberal in several areas of their livity. However, they are known, too, for their popular cultural dances, which are well organised and disciplined events. The organ counts several reggae artists among their members, one of whiom was Bob Marley, who also baptised as Berhan Selassie (Light of the Trinity) into the Ethiopian Orthodox Church before his passing.

v.   Other Associations

Many Rastafari are also baptised members of the Ethiopian Orthodox Church, even though there is resistance there against the wearing of dreadlocks and against I and I defence of His Imperial Majesty as the Returned Messiah, Christ in His Kingly Character, the Godhead. Nevertheless, the Rastafari zeal for its Ethiopian roots has a strong influence on Black interest in the Church from Afrikans in the Caribbean and the rest of the Diaspora. In fact, the establishment of the Church in Jamaica and Britain in the 1970s is a direct result of requests from the Rastafari community in general and members of the Ethiopian World Federation, Inc., in particular.

Recently there has been an effort to adapt the Church to the teachings of Rastafari through the formation of the *Ba Beta Kristiyan Haile Selassie I* (Church of Haile Selassie I) by a group of Brethren and Sistren under the leadership of elder

Ammanuel "Pinto" Foxe. *Ato**Foxe was instrumental in the earlier UBIO, and a branch of the EWF in England.

There are also those on the fringes of Rastafari, as well as those brothers and sisters known as Rasta-sympathisers. These include persons who are influenced and attracted by the livity of the *Movemant* but have not yet fully accepted its tenets.

In fact, many Rastafari of today first came to the *Movemant* via the conscious and inspirational message which members of the Faith put over in their melodious Niahbinghi inspired Jamaican reggae music. These messengers included, of course, the Right Honourable Bob (Robert) Nesta Marley (Berhan Selassie). Bob performed with fellow messengers, Bunny 'Wailer' Livingstone, Peter Tosh, The I-Threes - Rita Marley, Marcia Griffiths and Judy Mowatt, plus the Barrett brothers, and other members of the Wailers group, without whom he could not have gained the prominence he ultimately did.

High on the list of the early reggae messengers of Rastafari are also Daddy U-Roy, Big Youth, Prince Fari (the Psalms Master) The Abyssinians, Count Ossie and the Mystic Revelation of Rastafari, Burning Spear, Yabby U, Junior Byles, and the "Crown Prince of Reggae" Dennis Brown, among others. This tradition continues today with Rastafari stars such as the late great Garnet Silk, Sizzla, Buju Banton, and Ras Ites and Morgan Heritage, both youth bands from UK and USA, respectively. And of course, there's "The Messenger", Rastafari Luciano.

Outside of Jamaica, these artists are well known internationally, especially in Afrika. The inspiration to global Afrikan solidarity which Rasta and reggae music has brought was well

----

* *Ato* is 'Sir' or 'Mr' in Amharic.

appreciloved by Bro. President Robert Mugabe. He had proudly invited Rasta Brethren and Sistren of Bob Marley and the Wailers band to a special performance at Zimbabwe's Independence celebrations on 17 April 1980. This was indeed a

Early picture of *Ato* Ammanuel Foxe

spiritually motivating and uplifting experience for all - the massive live audience, as well as television viewers.

But now, a most unwelcome association with the *Movemant* is the advent of people who are not Rastas, nor sympathisers, but carry the outward covenant of Rastafari, namely the dreadlocks, and behave in a way to justify being called anti-Rasta tools of the devil. These are the *hypocrites and parasites*, and the *wolves in sheep's clothing* that Bob Marley and Dennis Brown sang about. Yet, undaunted, the true Rasta continues in his upright and 'upful' mission on behalf of the Ultimate Judge, Almighty Rastafari, for the judgement fire is not partial.

A true Rasta is known by "the words of his mouth and the meditation of his heart", as well as by the recommendation he gets and by the way he carries himself. Selah.

8.   DREADLOCKS AND BEARDS

Outside of Afrika, Dreadlocks Livity first re-emerged with the Hillsman in Jamaica. And although the Brothers and Sisters who came off the slave ships had dreadlocks in an early stage of growth, after months at sea, the locks offended the slave makers who had them cut off. The same applied to their language and culture. Dreadlocks became confirmed as a Family Livity at Leonard Howell's (Gong-g'un Guru Maragh's) Rastafari commune at Pinnacle. But dreadlocks and beards have been part of the Original Afrikan Man of RasTafari before Adam. Today, Rastafari nullify the Afrikan self-curse of the "bad hair" slavery mentality of too many of our people; I and I proudly maintain the "good wool" hair which Jah gave to us in our Ivine Afrikan dreadlocks character; as antennae to communicate with I and I.

The early Hillsman Rastas and the those at Pinnacle lived to nature in the freedom of the hills. They did not cut nor comb their beards or their wool, preferring only to wash and nurture them. As a result, the characteristic Afrikan dreadlocks developed. They were seen to be the same as those we later saw in pictures of Ethiopian Batawi priests and, after 1952, members of the Kenyan Mau Mau who were fighting for freedom from the British. Dreadlocks are also sanctioned by the Nazarite Law in the Bible - Numbers chapter 6. Man's growing of beard is sanctioned in Leviticus 19 v 27 and 21 v 5. Thus, the Rastaman is unshaved; he grows both his dreadlocks and his beard.

To maintain healthy dreadlocks, Rastafari wash them with herbal shampoo, pick and finger-comb them and oil them. After oiling the dreadlocks and the scalp, massage the scalp and your neck (or have them done for you!) to encourage a healthy flow of nutrient-rich blood to go to the head. Of course, exercise, sufficient sleep, proper nutrition and right behaviour are necessary for a rich circulation and good all-round health.

After bearing all manner of attacks and persecution from certain people in society who were fearful of the Rastafari message and their dreadlocks, society in general is now more used to them. Several not-Rasta people now enjoy the privilege of wearing dreadlocks and do so in comfort at the expense of Rasta. But dreadlocks are a responsibility for a conscious purpose. Therefore, dreadlocks, when worn, should be worn with discipline and with respect to Rastafari.

Dreadlocks were not meant for criminals to hide under the guise of Rastafari, as happened in the early days. Rasta dreadlocks are not tools for one's attempt to break into the reggae popular music scene. Nor are they meant for attracting white sexual, rental partners for fornication. Neither will they work as a guilt offering in one's aim to continue in their divided cultural and racial focus, and they certainly are not a "fashion ina Babylon".

Dreadlocks people should be able to respond to Rastafari greetings with an appropriate response and in a warm and heartical manner, rather than with guilt and embarrassment.

A one must respect the deep cultural, religious and mystical significance of Rastaman and Rastawoman's Sacredlocks. They are a covenant with our Jah, Haile Selassie I and with each other. They counteract the racial self-curse of those of who insult God and Man by frying, burning and straightening down their strong Afrikan wool. For although these misguided ones glorify the European type of hair, or fur, they tragically refer to their own wool as "bad hair," besides other negative and destructive approach to their Afrikan self. Rastafari dreadlocks are sacred and are, therefore, a reestablishment and reinforcement of Afrikan beauty and right living.

Although free-flowing dreadlocks are part of the natural righteous Man, many Rastaman, whilst living in an environment where divers un-natural and unrighteous practises flourish, and where atmospheric pollution is heavy, have to cover their locks in public. They remove their crown (hat) in public only for specially chosen reasons, or while in Rasta assemblies, unlike the Rasta Queens and Princesses who must always be properly crowned in public. This is part of their dressing in modesty, as well as the protection of their royal "bignity", personality, and their sexuality.

Finally, remember that nature and reason are against the combing of Afrikan wool, and even the so-called afro-combs cannot spare us the agony of a combing session. Nor can so-called shaving creams spare many Afrikan men the agony of "razor bumps" from ingrowing hair.

Mighty Dread: Ras Boanerges, co-founder of the Youth Black Faith and influential in developing the Niahbinghi Order and drumming.

Dreadlocks mean going forward to our Ancient Afrikan Livity of Righteousness and Naturalness; they are our ideal of **Black Beauty Without Vanity.** Selah.

9.   LOVE

Love conquers all; Love is Jah

With Love in your heart you fear no one. Love is Iternal while
everything else fades. Love is Jah, Haile Selassie I and I and I.
Love is accepting others even with their human weaknesses and
faults. ***"Knowledge* paves the way to *Love*, and Love in its
turn fosters *overstanding*, and leads one along the path of
great common achievements."**[14]
 Love and affection are different but complementary feelings,
yeah, deep things. Affection is the tender emotion which com-
plements Love. But Romance? That is "a fantastic exaggera-
tion or a distortion of the truth"[15] – an old Roman con-cept, confused with true love ina Babble-land. With romance you fall –
"fall in love?" But with true Love you rise – yes, rise like a dove,
and grow. Yeah.

To Love everyone is I aim, to **grow in Love** with someone is I
special gain.

Love is Justice & Responsibility

 Some people mistake selfishness and possessiveness for love.
Love is unselfish yet it is self, for, if you do not love yourself
you cannot Love others. But Love is not vain. Love is forgiving
while still maintaining your moral principles; it is compassion
with firmness. Love is doing unto others as you would like them
to do unto you, and so it means staking your claim and standing
up for your rights, if necessary. Love is getting to know one's
true self, that is, knowing the Ivine I within yourself and then
learning to recognise that I also in others. So, ultimately, Love
knows The Almighty Jah of Creation, Ras Tafari Haile Selassie
I and I and I. Give if you accept, accept only what is good, and
give only what you would accept.

Love is Inity

Love is not lust, and is not based on carnal desires. Love is not submission or an enforced loyalty to a downpressive bully. Although Love has no colour, race, nor nationality, yet Love begins at home, in I and I Inity. For, if love is expressed to out-siders only, it is then but a sham. Love created you and I to be one. *"I Am, because I and I are. And because I and I are, therefore I Am"*, in Love. Remember, Love wants Peace and Justice and Happiness for ALL.

When I Love I, I can Love I&I, and when I Love I&I, I know how to Love I and I and I - ALL I. For, true Love is cosmic and Iniversal and Iternal. True Love is the Almighty God, Haile Selassie I & I & I, Jah, RasTafari, Who wants Peace and Justice and Happiness for us ALL. Yeah...

... Love Is.

10. RASTAFARI HAIMANAT
(CREED & FOUNDATION PRINCIPLES OF RASTAFARI)

I and I know and affirm that the Almighty Jah!...
... RASTAFARI

i   IS HAILE SELASSIE I, King of kings and the Lord of lords, Conquering Lion of the tribe of Judah, Ilect of I-self and the Light of this world; Almighty, Almighty without an apology. Jah!

ii.   RASTAFARI is our I'ncient Livity, regenerating Life immortality. IAHBINGHI is the Law for the I'ncient Livity, Truth and Right, and Peace and Love, Ital Justice and Prosperity.

iii   MARRIAGE is the carriage for the Family life – the Hola Trinity in the Husband and the Children and the Mothering Wife.

iv.   CLEANLINESS is Ivineliness. To your gender you must dress. Wear clean clothes on a groomed clean body, wear them well with majesty.

v.   NATURALNESS is righteousness; the dread upon your head to the food upon your plate.

vi.   ITAL FOOD is natural food. Eat of the earth; leave the animals to birth.

vii.   SIX DAYS WORK and the seventh day for rest. Work and rest to enjoy the best.

viii.   ZION is on earth – say is AFRIKA the I Birth.

ix.   SPIRITUAL AND CULTURAL education is Inity for self and also the Nation.

x.   MARCUS, Marcus Mosiah Garvey. The Prophet who
        came with the great prophecy: RasTafari, Haile
        Selassie I, God of Ithiopia will save I and I.
        One RasTafari, One Righteous Aim, and One
        Destination to prosper our nation; REPATRIVATION
        for REGENERATION.

RASTAFARI have a trinity of methods or mode of expression in
proclaiming, inculcating, Ilibrating and affirming I and I Faith
(*Haimanat*).

There is the CREED (*Haimanat*) which reminds us of the foundation principles of our Faith.

There is the ANTHEM, which allows us to glorify and Ilibrate
our existence through song-chants.

Then there is the PRAYER of Iliverance, through which we
thank HIM for His Providence, ask HIM for forgivenness, for
gifts and special blessings, and affirm our intention to be obedient and loyalty to HIM.

11. THE INIVERSAL ETHIOPIAN ANTHEM

Ithiopia Thou Land of our Fathers
Thou Land where RasTafari loves to be
As the swift bee to hive suddenly gathers
Rastafari children are gathered to thee
With Our Green, Gold and Red floating over us
With our Emperor to shield us from wrongs
With Rastafari and our future before I & I
I & I hail Thee with chants and with songs.

CHORUS
Rastafari Bless our Negus, Negus I
Who keeps Ithiopia free (to advance)
To advance with Truth and Right (Truth and Right)
To advance with Love and Light (Love and Light)
With Righteousness leading
I & I haste to RasTafari and King
Imanity's pleading, One RasTafari for us all.

O Iternal RasTafari of the ages
Grant unto I & I sons that lead
Thy Wisemind as given to I & I Sages
When Afrika was sure in need
Thy Voice through the dim past has spoken
Ethiopians now stretch forth their hands
And by Thee shall all barriers be broken
And RasTafari Bless I & I dear Fatherland

Ithiopia, the tyrants are falling
Who smote thee upon thy knees
Thy children are heartically calling
From over Jah distant seas
RasTafari the Great One has heard I & I
He has noted our sighs and our tears
With His Spirit of Love He has stirred Us
To be one all through the coming years.

Origin of the Anthem

The Iniversal Ethiopian Anthem, chanted by Rastafari at their gatherings, is one aspect of I and I determination to value and promote the strength of Afrikan legacy, Inity, and traditions.

This anthem is essentially that which was adapted from a poem by Bro. Burrell and Bro. Rabbi Arnold Ford and resolved by Marcus Garvey's UNIA organisation, at their Conference of 1920, to be the anthem of the Afrikan race.

In this, and in our focus on repatrination, as well as I and I determination in maintaining Afrikan Black natural beauty, Inity, enterprise, and collective security, we are, surely, trodding on the road of "One Jah, One Aim and One Destiny" prosperity.

The Right Honourable Marcus Mosiah Garvey, Prophet, Visionary and Leader

12.   PRAYER IN RASTAFARI

ILIVERANCE PRAYER OF RASTAFARI

Princes and Princesses must come out of Babylon
Ithiopians now stretch forth their hands and hearts unto
RasTafari[16]
O Thou Ivine Majesty, Thy Irit come into I & I hearts
To dwell in the Path of Righteousness,
Help I & I to forgive
So that I & I may be forgiven
Teach I & I Love and Loyalty as it is in Mount Zion

Endow I & I with Thy Wisemind, Knowledge and Overstanding
to do Thy Will
Thy Blessing to I & I is: that the hungry be fed
The naked clothed, the sick nourished
The aged protected and the infants cared for.

Iliver I & I from the hands of I & I enemies
So that I & I may prove fruitful
Not only in this day, but also in the last days
When I & I enemies are past away and decayed
In the depth of the sea or in the depth of the earth
Or in the belly of the beast, or in the lake of fire
Give I & I all a place in Thy Righteous Kingdom, forIver and
Iver, O, Haile Selassie I, Jah, RasTafari.

What Is Prayer?

PRAYER can be individual or communal. However, it is essentially a personal communication / communion with Jah, the
Head Creator. To pray to Jah is to go deep within oneself and
speak with the Jah Within – *"Stand in awe, and sin not;*
commune with your own heart *upon your bed and be still.
Selah. Offer the sacrifices of righteousness and put your trust
in RasTafari."* (Psalms 2: 4+5). This means having a good, wor-

shipful relationship with Jah. Worship is Initation on Jah, giving HIM obedience, loyalty, adoration and Ivotion.

Prayer is acknowledging the Sovereignty of The Head Maker, thanking Him for knowing your <u>needs</u> and for satisfying them in the past, the present, and in the future (even without your knowledge). Prayer is also <u>the three Rs</u> - **researching** yourself, which is admitting to your good and your bad as one who's seeking perfection, then **repenting** of any wrong done, asking for forgiveness and committing to make **reparation (repair)**. You then declare your human <u>wants</u> and desires in a petition to HIM, Who is deep within your own heart. But you then have to trust in HIM (i.e. surrender to His Providence) with regards to the nature and timing of this Grant. We have to observe <u>the three Ps</u> - **patience, perseverance & prosperity.**

Rasta chant: "He never fails I yet, He never fails I yet; RasTafari never fails I yet. And everywhere I go I want the world to know, RasTafari never fails I yet."

Some Rastafari in Jamaica pray facing the East in order to face Ethiopia and the direction of the rising sun. In England, Ethiopia is to the south east. Niahbinghi assemblies pray facing each other in a circle around the altar.

A Prayer

Lord, lead I in the path of righteousness for Thy Name sake, O Abba I Jah RasTafari. Let I never be ashamed or afraid unduly. Help I to see, know and do that which I need for Your blessing. Regard the effort that I make to please You, O Jah RasTafari, more than the mistakes that I make. Bless I works to achieve I good. Guide, Protect, Bless and Prosper I, and I, and I, O, RasTafari. I beseech You. Aman. Selah.
May the words of I mouth, and the Initation of I heart, be acceptable in Thy Sight, O Fari.

13. "TEACHINGS OF HIS MAJESTY"

As Berhan Selassie (Bob Marley) said: "Give us The Teachings of His Majesty, for we nuh want nuh devil philosophy". The Words of HIM Emperor Haile Selassie I are **"THE NOW TESTAMANT"** - **our Comforter and Sustainer.** They provide a complete and modern worldview which encompasses the total human experience for development on the personal, as well as the collective level.

A. Sacred Writings

i. The Holy Bible (as Sighted by HIM)

"Ethiopia, an island of Christianity, is recorded in history as having received first the Old Testament, and then the New Testament, earlier than most of the countries of the world..."
(HIM Preface to the **Haile Selassie I Bible Translation**, 23 July 1961, plus p616 of "Selected Speeches"[17])

"We in Ethiopia have one of the oldest versions of the Bible. But however old the version may be, in whatever language it may be written, the Word remains one and the same. It transcends all boundaries of empires and all conceptions of race. It is eternal... For My part, I Glory in the Bible."

ii. Fetha Negast (The Law of the Kings)
This is the ancient law book of Ethiopia, which became the foundation for the modern constitutional legislation of Emperor Haile Selassie I's Government.

"The long and great history of Our country demonstrates

that Our people have always both administered and lived according to the Law. Our people were at first ruled by Mosaic law, but after the advent of Christianity to Ethiopia, they came later to be governed by the Fetha Negast – a work combining both spiritual and secular matters... it provided for Our people an invaluable source of legal principles. No modern legislation which does not have its roots in the custom of those whom it governs can have a strong foundation".

(HIM Preface to the national publication of the Fetha Negast, 29 August '68).

iii.   **Kebra Negast** (The Glory of Kings)
This is the ancient *I*story of the Ethiopian civilisation, which shows the Iscent of the Royal Dynasty from King Solomon and the Queen of Sheba. It records also the Ivinely ordained transfer of the Ark of the Covenant by their son, Menelik I, and the Falashas, from Jerusalem to the safe-keeping at Jah new Ivine place of abode on earth, the **New Jerusalem** at Aksum in Ethiopia.

"When we explore Ethiopian *I*story, the writings of the great historians convincingly prove to us that Ethiopia has greater antiquity than most countries and that she was honoured for wisdom and learning. Our Kebra Negast testifies that, when the Queen of Sheba went to Jerusalem to hear Solomon's wisdom, she presented to him various gifts she had brought. This proves to us Ethiopia's antiquity and her wisdom."
"Again, the fact that...the kings of Ethiopia, having crossed the sea, were governing the Arab country called Yemen demonstrates that... Ethiopia was a powerful nation."[18]
(Chapter 21, p121 Autobiography of Emperor Haile Selassie I Vol.1)

iv.   <u>More HIM Utterances: "The Now Testam*a*nt"</u>

a.   SERVE WITH HONESTY

"...It is evident that man in his lifetime is bound to encounter pleasure and hardship interchangeably. During trying moments one ought to overcome these painful periods with patience and perseverance, despite much suffering. On the other hand, when one is fully blessed with nature's endowments, one should not solely be given to pleasure but rather be self-restrained and useful. As excessive pleasure precipitates laziness, one should try to avoid being a victim of it..."
(P234 "Important Utterances", August 16, 1970)

b.   SPIRITUAL AND CULTURAL EDUCATION

"Specialisation tends towards diversification and division among human beings; spiritual and cultural education leads them back into unity on the national as well as on the personal level..." ("Speeches Delivered by HIM...1957-1959": July 19, 1957, p6.)

c.   INCAPABLE OF DESPAIR

"Our own life has demonstrated that We are incapable of despair. Men will die in defence of principles; men will sacrifice their all rather than compromise themselves and renounce that which distinguishes them from the beasts – their moral faculty. But if this force in men can but be awakened and focussed on the problems of each day, we shall, God willing, survive each day to the dawn of each tomorrow, and in this survival, guarantee to our children and our children's children a lifetime of peace and security, under justice and right, and under God."
(Selected Speeches, p187: September 3, 1961)

d.   IGNORANCE NO EXCUSE

"No judge could claim ignorance or poverty as an excuse for shortcomings in the administration of justice because he can neither shirk the responsibility entrusted to him by the Crown nor perjure his God-given conscience. It will be found that physical and material handicap, which are often short-lived and transitory, are not so harmful as finding one's self faced with a guilty conscience. WHENEVER CONFLICT ARISES BETWEEN MATERIAL AND SPIRITUAL VALUES, THE CONSCIENCE PLAYS AN IMPORTANT ROLE."

(Selected Speeches, p418: August 24, 1961)

e.   PROGRESS MUST BE MORAL

"One cannot deny that in former times man's life had been one of toil and hardship. It is correct to say, therefore, that modern civilisation and the progress of science have greatly improved man's life and have brought comfort and ease in their trail. But civilisation can serve man both for good as well as for evil purposes... It has invariably brought great dividends to those who use it for good purposes while it has always brought incalculable harm and damnation to those who use it for evil purposes.

To make our will obedient to good influences and to avoid evil, therefore, is to show the greatest wisdom. In order to follow this aim one must be guided by religion. Progress without religion is just like a life surrounded by unknown perils and can be compared to a body without a soul. It is only when the human mind is guided by religion and morality that man can acquire the necessary vision to put all his ingenious inventions and contrivances to really useful and beneficial purposes.

HIM Emperor Haile Selassie I, Man of Knowledge and of Books
"There is no end to learning" (HIM)

It is important that spiritual advancement must keep pace with material advancement... Only then shall we be able to acquire that absolute inner calm so necessary to our well-being." (Selected Speeches, p662: April 5, 1948)

f. EDUCATIONAL

"Learning and profound knowledge nurture noble character and impart wisdom. The family unit and educational establishments have great responsibilities in these endeavours for they are the basis of national progress and prosperity...You should be well aware of the fact that it is not mere academic achievement that is expected of you. Your knowledge and training, unless put to proper and practical use, will be wasted like hoarded money and you will be no better in this regard than the uneducated. "

"Education is the gateway to everlasting enlightenment ... THERE IS NO END TO LEARNING..." (Important Utterances: p271, Aug.1, '71; College of Public Health, Jul 3, '70)

g. ADDRESSING JAMAICAN HOUSES OF PARLIAMENT

"The relations...between the people of Jamaica and the people of Ethiopia are deep and abiding... a bond of brotherhood. The people of Jamaica, by and large, have originated in Afrika.

It is quite true that a country can achieve material progress alone.* However... international co-operation tends to quicken the pace of progress of individual countries. This is another area for us to think about and see in what way we

----

* i.e. by themselves

can further expand relations between us. From another fundamental point of view, this is why the Organisation of Afrikan Unity (OAU)[19] has been established. Since there is an identity of interest, We have attempted to include Jamaica also, so that we can carry this weight in the council of nations... and be in a position to quicken the pace of development of the individual member countries of the OAU.

I would broadly say wherever there is Afrikan blood there is a basis for greater unity."
(Selected Speeches, p140: April, 1966)

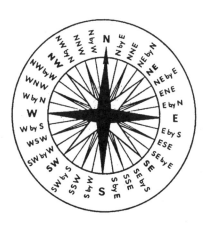

B.   Clarifying Some Previous "Testamants"

i.   The Ten Commandments in the Bible (Exodus 20:2-17 & Deuteronomy 5:6-21+29) are good codes of practice for all peoples. RasTafari requires that we keep them, always. People who try to use the New Testament to interpret to the contrary are misrepresenting the stated Laws of God for their own reasons. Deuteronomy 5 verse 29 states: "O that there were such an heart in them, that they would fear me, and **keep all my Commandments always,** that it might be well with them, and with their children for ever!" They are:

Ethiopian Priests carrying the Tablets of The Ten Commandments from the Ark of the Covenant.

1. Thou shalt have no other gods before me.

2. Thou shalt not make unto thee any graven image, or any like-ness of any thing that is in heaven above, or that is in the earth beneath, or that is in the water under the earth; Thou shalt not bow down thyself to them, nor serve them. For I the Lord thy God am a jealous God, visiting the iniquity of the fathers upon

the children unto the third and fourth generation of them that hate me; and showing mercy unto thousands of them that love me, and **keep my Commandments.**

3. Thou shalt not take the Name of the Lord thy God in vain; for the Lord will not hold him guiltless that taketh His name in vain.

4. Remember the Sabbath day, to keep it holy. Six days shalt thou labour, and do all thy work; but the seventh day is the Sabbath of the Lord they God, in it thou shalt not do any work, thou, nor thy son, nor thy daughter, thy manservant, nor thy maidservant, nor thy cattle, not thy stranger that is within thy gates. For in six days the Lord made heaven and earth, the sea, and all that is in them, and rested the seventh day; wherefore, the Lord blessed the Sabbath day, and hallowed it.

5. Honour thy Father and thy Mother, that thy days may be long upon the land which the Lord thy God giveth thee.

6. Thou shalt not kill (**meaning**, you shall not murder).

7. Thou shalt not commit adultery.*

8. Thou shalt not steal.

9. Thou shalt not bear false witness against thy neighbour (**meaning**, our fellow).

10. Thou shalt not covet thy neighbour's house; thou shalt not covet thy neighbour's wife, nor his manservant, nor his maidservant, nor his ox, nor his ass, nor anything that is thy neighbour's.

----

* See also page 49

ii.   Matthew 7:1: **"Judge not that ye be not judged."**

Some people wrongly wish to interpret this to suggest that we must not judge, meaning that they want to do whatever they wish and not be called to judgement. Now, logically, the highly intelligent Being of Jesus the Christ, in His "Sermon on the Mount" would not tell people not to use their powers of discernment, to judge good from bad, wrong from right, or dangerous from safe.

Otherwise, He would not be able to direct us: "*...If thy brother trespass against thee* (if he does you wrong) *go and tell him his fault privately...But if he will not listen, take one or two more witnesses... And if he shall neglect to hear them, tell it unto the church: but if he neglect to hear the church, let him be unto you as an heathen man and a publican.*"   That is judgement! (Matthew 18:15 -17).

What the Christ meant was what he said later on, in chapter 7, verse 2: *"For with what judgement ye judge, ye shall be judged..."* Clearly, he means that you should *"Do unto others as you would have them do unto you"* (and yours) (Matthew 7v12). This means that you should judge by the same measure that you yourself would like to be judged. So judge fairly, with justice.

iii.   **"God is No Respecter of Persons"**

This means that God does not regard personality cults. He gives judgement and recompense to all people, according to their worth, not according to their personality or their man made status.

Genesis 4 v 4-5 states: *"And the Lord had respect unto Abel and to his offering; but unto Cain and to his offering He had no respect."* Cain had done well, Abel hadn't. And there is a similar example in 2 Chronicles 19:7.

Proverbs 24:23 states: *"...It is not good to have respect of persons in judgement."* Leviticus 19:15 has a similar counsel.

Acts10:34: *"...Of a truth I perceive that God is no respecter of persons."* This is similar to Romans 2:11.

1 Peter 1:17: *"...The Father, without respect of persons, judgeth according to every man's work."*

iv.   "The Love of Money is the Root of All Evil"

It is not merely money which is the root of all evil, which is often said. It is the **love** of money which is stated in the Bible as being the root of all evil (1 Timothy 6v10).

The *Kwerata Resu*, ancient Ethiopian picture-treasure
of Yesus Christus in His Afrikan dreadlocked appearance

110

v.   **The Date of the Birth of Yesus Christus**
      Genna (Christmas)

Points to remember:
*   ABIB (**April**) was the start of the biblical year.

*   HIGH PRIEST ZACHARIAH'S ATONEMENT SERVICE:
a. The High Priests took turns at atonement service.
b. Services are the 10th Day of 7TH MONTH (**October**).
c. Zacharia's turn was called the course of Abia. (Luke 1:5-10; Leviticus 16:29-34 + Numbers 29:7-11)

*   COUSINS ELISABETH'S & MARY'S PREGNANCIES WERE 6 MONTHS APART (John was 6 months Jesus' senior).
The History:
IN OCTOBER, during Zachariah's atonement service, he visioned the birth of his son, John the Baptist. He then went home and gave the seed of John to his wife, Elisabeth. (Luke 1:11-13+19).

Six months later, IN APRIL, the Blessed Mary became pregnant with Yesus Christus. (Luke 1: 26-36).

Allow 9 months on top of April gives a JANUARY Birth for Yesus. By detailed lunar and stellar calculations of the priests, the 7th of January is arrived at.

WHY RASTAFARI CELEBRATE GENNA:
It is an acknowledgement of the good works of Yesus Christus.

He's a good example of one who has attained high spiritual illumination and advancement.
It is in respect to a part of ancient Ethiopian Tradition.
Rastafari respect the Christ *trodition* which our Parents took in

their survival, and through which we've found the Revealed Father, HIM Emperor Haile Selassie I.

THE LORD'S PRAYER: *ABATACHIN HOY* (THE OUR FATHER)
Our Father, Who Art in Zion,
Hallowed be Thy Name
Thy Kingdom come, Thy Will be done
On Earth as it is in Zion
Give us this day, our daily bread
And forgive us our trespasses
As we forgive them that trespass against us
Lead us not into temptation
But Iliver us from evil
For Thine is the Kingdom, the Power and the Glory
Foriver and Iver, Aman.   (Matthew 6 verses 9 - 13)

HIM: prayerful & healing.
"And Jah made light out of the darkness."

112

14.   BEYOND THE 21ST CENTURY

Today, the world is seeing that despite the economic, technological and military might that nations might possess, the less equipped but determined peoples, who are convinced they are fighting for justice and liberty, can still find ways to cause those who they see as the mighty bully to feel insecure and afraid. It is David and Goliath all over again.

Whatever the truth is behind the so-called "9/11" (September 11th, 2001) event, this bombing of the twin towers in New York, USA, was a terror attack which shows that the possibility of the weaker person overcoming the one stronger in might is an eternal reality. It is not might which is right, but right which is might. In the 1935-1941 European war against Ethiopia, their conscience allowed them, through Italy, to use prohibited chemical warfare against us. But today, they live in terror of those same chemical weapons coming back at them. What you do...

The life principles of Rastafari and all peoples of good morals, which state that truth, right and justice are the only salvation for mankind, are daily manifested on the personal and the collective levels. But too many people continue to turn a blind eye to the truth. In the eyes of I and I, the wicked continue to fight against the truth which Rastafari defend. They waste their time and energy in trying to discredit Rasta philosophy at every least opportunity. Although there are apparent contradictions and errors in all of the other faiths and religions, they ignore them in preference to attacking Rasta.

For three years, around the Coronation or Earthday anniversaries of HIM, between the years 1992 and 2000, the world's propaganda media reported the so-called discovery of the bones of His Majesty, and their intended re-burial ceremony. But each time, these bones turned out to be the wrong size!

Prior to this, after His Majesty's Disappearance in 1975, the big mockery against Rastafari was to say, "See Rasta, yuh god is dead." After the revolution in 1974 and the subsequent mystical Disappearance of His Majesty, they claimed that He was murdered in 1975, and so, they hoped this would demoralise and destroy the Rasta Movemant. But, as Psalms 2 says: *"Why do the heathen rage, and the people imagine a vain thing? He that sitteth in the heavens shall laugh: the Lord shall have them in derision."* And as Bob Marley said, "Jah lives, children, yeah!" I and I are proof of that.

Rastafari has remained focussed. We place the greatest emphasis on balancing self-help with the expectancy of help from HIM. It is with His Guidance that Rastafari will *I*tinue prosperous in our self-help programmes of economics and administration, education, communication, security, food, transportation, clothing, building, health, music and the arts, sports and recre*n*ation, and science and technology. Because He is not readily visible today, since His rising from His Throne in 1974, I and I have to look deeper into I and I selves in order to communicate with HIM. Because of HIM we see the light of Love in Justice and Godliness, knowing that if we do not love ourselves we cannot love others.

In this Revelation, "is not Jah alone will bear the burden", and because of HIM our individual burden is lighter. Praise Jah.

The Royal Example of HIM and His Queen as presented here is, surely, Good, Better and Best for I and I, and Imanity. It is progress, surely, above the state which "men and people" have fallen into. In the early days of Rastafari re-emergence in Jamaica, the hatred and animosity of the wider society towards Rastafari did not allow woman to freely and openly practice the Faith with their manfolk. It was, therefore, the role of the Rastaman to take to the frontline of the battles in safeguarding the Faith on behalf of the Rastafari Family. Hence, the

Rastawoman was not so visible. However, today, the Rastawoman, like Empress Menen to Emperor Haile Selassie I, stands as a full partner with the Rastaman. They make a positive impact on society with their conscious recognition of the special, complementary role of the woman, and of the family in the welfare of the individual and the society.

The Rastaman and the Rastawoman have borne the hard times with HIM and so we deserve to "fultake" of the Godly rewards with HIM, too. We have His Majestic Example to follow, and we are more certain that, however ones and ones want to take it, RasTafari lives ForIver. He is Everliving. Likewise, because of HIM and His Queen, I and I have remembered our Heritage as Princes & Princesses and Kings & Queens. I and I are now on the road to remembering how to be Gods & Godesses, too, to share Iternity with HIM in Paradise (Zion); I and I blessed survival in prosperity.

All Praises to The I and I and I, Emperor Haile Selassie I, Jah RasTafari.

Their Royal Majesties and Family

115

ENDNOTES

1. (pages 4+6) The first formal written constitution of Ethiopia was Granted by HIM on 16 July 1931, later revised, expanded and Granted again by HIM on 4 November 1955. See also page 39 and 412 of "Selected Speeches".

2. (page 13) Also called kerosene.

3. (page 34) Confirmed in the Guinness Book of Records, and *New Lands* by Charles Hoy Fort.

4. (page 35) Regent: One who is appointed to rule in place of the monarch who's a minor, or who's ill, incapable, absent, or otherwise has that need. Ras Tafari was Regent first for His cousin, Lidj Iyasu, then for Empress Zawditu (Emperor Menelik's daughter).

5. (page 37) On page 48, chapter 4 of "The Ethiopians" (1973 ed.) the translator of vol. 1 of HIM Autobiography, E Ullendorff spoke true when he wrote:
   "The Abyssinian influence on pre-Islamic Arabia is
   reflected in a fair number of Ethiopian loan-words in Arabic."

6. (page 38) See note 1.

7. (page 39) See note 5.

8. (page 40) The Organisation of Afrikan Unity was changed (9th July 2002) to the Afrikan Union.

9. (page 50) Fetha Negast - see also page 100.

10. (page 55) Sirach (also called Ecclesiasticus) is a Book in the Ethiopian Bible (which has 81 books). It is also in the Revised Standard Version Bible, and the Apocrypha.

11. (pages 55+59) Up to date research carried out by the Jewish and Muslim faiths into "unclean" additions to commercial foods is useful for I and I. Insights into their nutritional laws are given in: *Introduction to Judaism* by Isidore Fishman, and *The Muslim Woman's Handbook* by Huda Khattab.

12. (page 61) OAU - see note 8.

13. (page 62) Western leap years are exactly divisible by 4 (e.g. 2004 divided by 4 = 501 exactly - no remainder).

14. (page 92) HIM Utterance.

15. (page 92) The Pocket Oxford Dictionary definition,1979.

16. (page 98) This Prayer was inspired by Psalms 68v31, and by "The Shepherd's Prayer" by Atlyi (from Shepherd Robert Atlyi Rogers' *"The Holy Piby"*) and by Rastafari Inspiration.

17. (page 100) Selected Speeches is also published as "The Third Testament – The Ilect Verses of Emperor Haile Selassie I" - see booklist.

18. (page 101) Jerusalem was once one of the provinces of the Ethiopian Empire.

19. (page 106) OAU - see note 8.

FOR FURTHER READING*:

The Autobiography of Emperor Haile Selassie I, "My Life and Ethiopia's Progress"
(a) volume 1, translated by E Ullendorff, re-published by Research Associates School Times Publications, Jamaica;
(b) vol.2, translated by Ezekiel Gebissa; edited and anotated by Harold Marcus, published by Research Associates School Times Publications, Jamaica.

Selected Speeches of HIM Haile Selassie I. Also published as "The Third Testament – The Ilect Verses of Emperor Haile Selassie I", by Headstart Printing & Publishing Co. (Ja).

Important Utterances of HIM Emperor Haile Selassie I, Jah Rastafari, volumes 1 & 2. Excerpted booklets by Voice of Rasta Publication.

The Kebra Negast
(a) The Queen of Sheba and Her Only Son Menyelik: The Kebra Negast; translated by E Wallis Budge
(b) The Kebra Negast; translated by Miguel F Brooks, Red Sea Press, Inc.

The Fetha Negast, publ. by Frontline Publications.

Holy Bible

Philosophy and Opinions of Marcus Garvey - (a) volumes 1 and 2, Publ. by Athenaeum (NY);
(b) Vol.3, pub. Collier-Macmillan as **More Philosophy & Opinions of Marcus Garvey.**

Health and Nutrition: A Rastafari Perspective by Kwende Anbessa-Ebanks, publ. by Kwemara Publications.

Ras Tafari Educational Pack, publ. by the Ethiopian World Federation, Inc. RRC.

Report on The Rastafari Movement in Kingston, Jamaica, M G Smith, Roy Augier & Rex Nettleford, publ. University of the West Indies.

Revelation: The Last Prophecy by Sheba Amlak, publ. by The New Zion.

A Historical Report: The Rastafari Movement in England by Norman W Adams, publ. by GWA Works.

The Culture, History and Universal Spread of Rastafari: Two Essays, by E S P McPherson (B.A Hons), publ. by Black International Iyahbinghi Press (Ja).

Jahug magazines

Rastafari Speaks newspaper

The Promised Key by G G Maragh (Leonard P Howell), introduced by E S P McPherson, republished by A& B Publishers Group.

* AVAILABILITY NOTE:

Some books which are out of print at the time of writing might be available through ones and ones' public library or national deposit library.

ONE RASTAFARI

VERSE 1

One RasTafari, only Rastafari
Always gonna trod that Way
One Righteous Aim, yes, I and I the Same
We're moving out of Babilon
One Destination, Ina Ityopya
Peace and Love and Imony
One Destination, Ina Ityopya
Peace and Love and Imony

CHORUS

So you fi
Tell them, we're moving in a higher Realm
And you fi
Tell them, we'll never be no slave again
Yes tell them, we're moving in a higher Realm
And you fi
Tell them, we'll never be no slave again
For we have One RasTafari, only RasTafari
Always gonna trod that Way

VERSE 2

Mi sey fi

One RasTafari, only Rastafari
Always gonna trod that Way
One Righteous Aim, yes, I and I the Same
We're moving out of Babilon
One Destination, Ina Ityopya
Peace and Love and Imony
One Destination, Ina Ityopya
Peace and Love and Imony

His Majesty's Favourite Portrait

INDEX

BOLD index items are topics of HIM Utterances entered in this Book.

STUDY NOTES

GUIDANCE AND ITECTION; STAY BLESSED